I LIVED THERE BEFORE THE SCIENCE

Tina Ketch

I LIVED THERE BEFORE THE SCIENCE

This book is a work of reflective narrative and remembrance. It is not intended as historical documentation, scientific instruction, or medical advice. Any interpretations are offered as personal reflection and experiential insight.

ISBN: 979-8-9937372-8-7
eISBN: 979-8-9937372-9-4

For information, inquiries, or permissions, contact:

https://TinaKetch.com
TinaKetch@me.com
https://YouTube.com/TinaKetch

DEDICATION

Video provides a powerful way to help you prove your point. When you click Online Video, you can paste in the embed code for the video you want to add. You can also type a keyword to search online for the video that best fits your document.

To make your document look professionally produced, Word provides header, footer, cover page, and text box designs that complement each other. For example, you can add a matching cover page, header, and sidebar. Click Insert and then choose the elements you want from the different galleries.

Themes and styles also help keep your document coordinated. When you click Design and choose a new Theme, the pictures, charts, and SmartArt graphics change to match your new theme. When you apply styles, your headings change to match the new theme.

Save time in Word with new buttons that show up where you need them. To change the way a picture fits in your document, click it and a button for layout options appears next to it. When you work on a table, click where you want to add a row or a column, and then click the plus sign.

Reading is easier, too, in the new Reading view. You can collapse parts of the document and focus on the text you want. If you need to stop reading before you reach the end, Word remembers where you left off - even on another device.

I LIVED THERE BEFORE THE SCIENCE

A MEMORY SCENE

I remember the sound before I remember the place.

It wasn't loud. It didn't demand attention. It arrived the way breath does, already inside me before I noticed it had come. The bells did not ring at us. They moved through us, gently adjusting something that had drifted out of alignment.

When they sounded, my chest softened. My thoughts slowed. The tight places in my body released without effort, as though they had been waiting for permission.

We did not call it healing. We called it living.

The towers stood throughout the town, placed with such care that no space was untouched by their reach. Each bell was tuned, not only to the others, but to the streets, the water, the air itself. When they moved together, the entire town breathed as one body.

I remember standing still when they rang, not because I was told to, but because my body knew it was the right response.

Light followed sound.

The windows, what you would now call church windows, though they belonged to everyone, shifted with the sun. They were alive in their own way, responding to angle, season, and time of day. Color poured through them, not randomly, but with intention. Gold for clarity. Blue for rest. Green for balance. Red for grounding.

When the light passed through the glass and touched my skin, it felt warm, but not hot. It carried information. My body recognized it the way a plant recognizes water.

We learned early that nothing in our world was decorative.

Everything worked.

The buildings were quiet. No smoke. No wires. No engines straining against the air. Energy was not produced, it was collected. Drawn from the space above us and the earth beneath our feet. It moved without friction, without waste.

At night, the town glowed softly, as though remembering the sun long after it had set.

Illness was rare, not because bodies were perfect, but because imbalance was addressed before it became pain. When someone felt unwell, they didn't isolate. They walked. They listened. They sat near water or beneath the windows when the light was right. Often, that was enough.

We understood that the body speaks quietly at first.

I remember the streets, not straight, but purposeful. Curving gently, guiding movement rather than forcing it. Water ran alongside many of them, carrying sound and reflection. Children played without hurry. Elders watched without fear.

No one was rushed.

Time did not press down on us then.

I did not know this world would disappear. I did not know the bells would one day be silenced, the windows stripped of their purpose, the knowledge renamed something else so it could be dismissed.

I only knew that life felt whole.

And when I left that place, when the remembering went dormant, something in me promised not to forget entirely.

That promise is why I am writing now.

Because I lived there before the science.

And so did we.

THE BELLS

DEEPENED MEMORY

The bells were not made to be heard from far away.

They were made to be felt.

Each one was cast with intention, its shape, thickness, and alloy chosen not for volume, but for response. When struck, the sound did not rush outward. It bloomed. The vibration unfolded slowly, like a ripple expanding across still water.

We never used the word frequency, though we understood it.

The bells were tuned to the human body.

Some were lower, meant to settle the chest and calm the breath. Others carried a higher tone that cleared the mind and sharpened focus. There were bells for rest, bells for renewal, bells that gently ushered the day toward sleep.

They never rang randomly.

Each tone corresponded with the hour, the season, and the collective state of the town. On days when grief moved through us, yes, even then, the bells sounded differently. Slower. Deeper. As though they were listening to us before they spoke.

I remember how my body responded before my thoughts caught up.

When the morning bells rang, my spine straightened without effort. When the evening tones arrived, my shoulders softened, and the day released its grip. Children grew calm without being told. Animals stilled and rested.

No one argued with the bells.

Not because we were obedient, but because they were kind.

The towers were placed where earth currents crossed, though we did not speak of lines or grids. We simply knew the ground hummed differently there. When the bells rang together, their sounds met in the air above the town, weaving into something larger than any single tone.

That woven sound held us.

Visitors often noticed it first. They would stop walking mid-step, hands moving to their chest or throat, surprised by an emotion they couldn't name. Some cried without sadness. Others laughed softly, embarrassed, as though caught remembering something personal.

We never explained.

Understanding came through experience.

I remember once asking an elder what would happen if the bells stopped.

She smiled gently, the way one does when answering a question too large for its moment.

"They won't," she said. "Not while we remember how to listen."

Much later, I would understand what she meant.

Because when the bells were finally taken down, it wasn't the silence that hurt most.

It was the way people forgot how to feel whole without being told.

And still, when I hear certain tones now, when a sound moves through my chest just right, I know the bells are not gone.

They are waiting.

THE WINDOWS OF LIVING LIGHT

DEEPENED MEMORY

The windows were never still.

They appeared that way to those who didn't know how to look, but we felt their movement long before we saw it. They responded to the sun as naturally as skin responds to warmth. As the day shifted, so did they, quietly adjusting their angles, their depth, the way color passed through them and into the world.

Light was not allowed to enter our buildings by accident.

Each window was placed with precision, aligned not only to the sun's path, but to the rhythms of the body. Morning light entered differently than afternoon light. Winter carried a slower tone. Summer light was brighter, more expansive.

We did not decorate with color.

We prescribed it.

Gold for clarity of thought. Blue for rest and restoration. Green for balance and healing. Violet for insight and remembrance.

When the light touched the body, it didn't blind or overwhelm. It settled. It moved through muscle and bone as though the body had been waiting for that exact shade all along.

I remember standing beneath one of the great windows when my thoughts felt tangled. I didn't know why I went there, only that my feet carried me. The light passed through amber and pale blue before reaching my face, and something inside my mind loosened.

No words were spoken.

None were needed.

The buildings that held these windows were open to all. Some gathered there in the morning to align themselves for the day. Others came in the late hours, when the light was gentler, preparing the body for rest. Children wandered in and out freely, often lying on the floors where color pooled like water.

No one worried about productivity.

We trusted restoration.

The glass itself was unlike anything now remembered. It was not flat. Not fixed. It held depth, as though layers of intention were embedded within it. When sound from the bells passed through the windows, the light responded, subtle shifts in hue and intensity that only the body could fully interpret.

Sound and light spoke to each other.

We simply lived between them.

I remember elders teaching us not to stare directly at the light, but to let it reach us indirectly. "The body listens better than the eyes," they would say. And it was true. The light worked even when we weren't watching.

Especially then.

There were times, rare, but unforgettable, when the light changed suddenly. During storms. During collective grief. During moments of great joy. The windows responded, altering their colors as though acknowledging what moved through us.

They were not intelligent in the way machines are now imagined.

They were attuned.

When the old knowledge faded, the windows remained, at least for a while. People still admired their beauty. They called them sacred. They argued about their meaning.

But beauty without understanding is a fragile thing.

Eventually, the angles were altered. The glass was replaced or covered. The buildings repurposed. The light entered without intention again.

And yet, when sunlight passes through colored glass now, when it lands on skin just right, something in me remembers.

That light once healed us.

Not because it was miraculous.

But because it was understood.

QUIET POWER - FREE ENERGY WITHOUT FIRE

DEEPENED MEMORY

Power in our world was never something you noticed.

That may be the hardest thing to explain now. There was no noise announcing it, no heat rising from it, no smell of fuel or burning. It did not demand space or attention. It simply existed, present in the way air is present, doing its work without needing to be seen.

We did not "generate" energy.

We received it.

The towers, the rooftops, the waterways, all of them were designed to gather what was already moving around us. The sky carried charge. The earth carried current. Water carried memory. Our structures listened and responded.

When energy moved, it did so gently, without resistance. There was no strain in it. No push. No force.

Nothing in our town fought against nature.

That was the difference.

At night, lamps glowed without flame. Their light was soft, steady, and cool. Homes were warm without fire. Tools moved without effort. Even the bells, so carefully tuned, were supported by this silent power, never draining, never consuming.

Children grew up without fearing darkness.

We trusted the systems because they were built on harmony, not extraction.

I remember once asking how it all worked. I was young and curious, wanting answers the way children do. An elder placed her hand on the ground and then over my heart.

"Feel that?" she asked.

I did.

"That's the same thing," she said.

That was the extent of the explanation.

There were no engines to break, no fuel to ration, no dependence that made us anxious. Energy was shared, not owned. No one profited from it. No one controlled it.

Because control was unnecessary.

When people speak now of progress, they often mean speed. But we did not measure advancement by how fast something could move or how much it could produce. We measured it by how little harm it caused, how gently it allowed life to continue.

When this knowledge began to fade, it didn't vanish all at once. Systems were altered "for safety." Access became restricted. Maintenance required permissions. Eventually, the quiet power was replaced with something louder, more aggressive, more profitable.

People learned to tolerate discomfort and called it normal.

I remember the first time a machine roared where there had once been silence.

My body recoiled before my mind understood why.

Because the power we once lived with never hurt our ears.

Or the earth.

Or each other.

THE TOWN AS A LIVING HEALER

DEEPENED MEMORY

We did not build the town on the land.

We built it with the land.

Every street, every curve, every open space was shaped with the understanding that the earth itself was alive and responsive. We didn't impose order, we followed it. The ground spoke quietly, and we learned how to listen with our feet, our breath, our posture.

Movement mattered.

The streets were never straight for long. They curved gently, guiding the body rather than forcing it. Walking through the town felt different than walking elsewhere. The pace slowed naturally. Breathing deepened without instruction.

Even visitors noticed.

"This place makes me feel lighter," they would say, surprised by their own words.

We smiled, because that was the point.

Water flowed everywhere, not contained, not hidden. It ran alongside paths, through courtyards, beneath gathering places. The sound of it softened the nervous system, long before anyone would give such a thing a name.

Fountains weren't ornamental.

They were regulators.

Each one shaped sound and movement differently. Some energized. Some calmed. Some helped people release emotions they didn't yet have language for. It wasn't uncommon to see someone sit by the water, eyes closed, letting tears come without shame.

No one asked why.

We understood that emotion moves like water, it needs space.

There were places where the town felt especially alive. Crossings where people lingered without knowing why. Courtyards where arguments softened and laughter returned. These weren't accidents. The town itself had pressure points, just as the body does.

We knew where to go when something felt off.

There were no hospitals as you know them now. Healing wasn't centralized, it was distributed. If someone felt unwell, they walked. They rested in certain spaces. They stood beneath the windows when the light was right. They listened to the bells when the tones shifted toward restoration.

Often, that was enough.

When it wasn't, others came, not as authorities, but as companions. They listened. They placed hands on backs or shoulders, not to fix, but to support. Touch was understood as communication, not intervention.

No one was rushed to be better.

We trusted the body's intelligence.

Children grew strong without being pushed. Elders aged without being isolated. Grief was shared. Joy was communal. No one was expected to endure life alone.

The town held us.

That is what I miss most, not the technology, not the beauty, but the feeling of being carried by something larger than myself.

When the systems that supported this way of life began to disappear, people didn't fall ill immediately. At first, they simply felt tired. Disconnected. Less patient. More anxious.

They blamed themselves.

They didn't yet realize the town was no longer helping them hold their balance.

Because when a place stops caring for its people, the people must carry everything alone.

And we were never meant to.

WHEN SOUND AND LIGHT FELL OUT OF HARMONY

THE FIRST FRACTURE

No one announced that anything was wrong.

That is how it began.

The bells still rang. The windows still glowed. The town still moved and breathed as it always had. And yet, something underneath it all had shifted, like a note played just slightly off-key. Most people didn't notice at first. The body sensed it before the mind could name it.

I remember the day clearly, though nothing remarkable seemed to happen.

The morning bells rang on time, but my chest didn't soften the way it usually did. The sound passed through me without settling. I stood still longer than normal, waiting for my body to respond.

It didn't.

I told myself I was tired.

Others did the same.

The windows still carried color, but the light felt thinner somehow. Sharper at certain angles. When it touched my skin, it warmed me, but it no longer spoke. The quiet communication between sound and light had begun to slip out of sync.

No one said the word broken.

Instead, new words appeared.

"Improvement." "Efficiency." "Standardization."

People began measuring what had never needed to be measured before.

The bells were adjusted, not retuned, but restrained. Their range narrowed. Certain tones were deemed unnecessary. Too emotional. Too disruptive. Someone decided that consistency mattered more than responsiveness.

The windows were fixed in place.

That change was subtle, but devastating.

They could no longer adjust to the seasons or the needs of the body. Light still entered, but without nuance. Color became aesthetic instead of medicinal. People admired it, took comfort in its beauty, unaware of what had been lost.

The town still healed, but more slowly.

People lingered longer by the fountains. Walked farther than before to feel balanced. Children grew restless without knowing why. Elders grew quieter, carrying a sadness they could not explain.

And then came the explanations.

Some said the old ways were inefficient. Others said they were impractical. A few said they were dangerous.

Fear crept in wearing the clothes of reason.

I remember overhearing a conversation, two voices low and urgent, speaking of control, of predictability, of systems that could be owned rather than shared. They spoke as though harmony were a liability.

I remember my body reacting before my mind did.

A tightening in my throat. A pressure behind my eyes. A grief that arrived too early to be understood.

That was when I realized:

The town was still standing. The technology was still functioning. But the relationship had changed.

We were no longer listening.

And when a civilization stops listening to what sustains it, forgetting follows naturally.

THE DAY THE BELLS FELL SILENT

NOT ALL AT ONCE

The silence did not arrive suddenly.

That is the lie people tell later, when memory becomes easier if it is sharp and dramatic. But this silence was patient. It entered slowly, almost kindly, so no one would panic. So no one would resist too quickly.

At first, only certain bells were quiet.

Those tuned to rest. Those meant to soften grief. Those that spoke to the body more than the mind.

They said the tones were unnecessary. Too subtle. Too difficult to regulate. Some claimed people reacted unpredictably to them, felt too much, remembered too deeply.

The remaining bells were allowed to ring.

For a while.

But without their companions, their voices felt lonely. Incomplete. The woven sound that once held the town together began to unravel. People noticed they woke more tired than before. Sleep grew shallow. Dreams faded.

We adapted.

That was our mistake.

The windows no longer responded when the bells rang. Sound passed through them without changing the light. The conversation between vibration and color, once so effortless, was broken.

Buildings still stood, but they no longer listened.

I remember the day a bell was removed.

There were no crowds. No ceremony. Just a small group of workers, efficient and quiet. The tower looked naked without it, hollow, like a body missing an organ no one believed it needed.

When the bell was lifted away, something inside me dropped.

I felt it in my stomach first.

Then my throat.

I wanted to speak, to object, to ask why, but no words came. It was as though the very frequencies that once supported expression had been withdrawn.

Others felt it too, though few acknowledged it. Some became irritable. Others withdrew. A few grew ill, and no one understood why the familiar remedies no longer worked as they once had.

The town tried to heal itself.

But without its full voice, it struggled.

Eventually, the bells were declared relics. Symbols. Decorative remnants of an outdated system. Some were melted down. Others were shipped away, repurposed, or locked behind walls where no one could hear them.

Silence settled, not empty, but heavy.

That was when time began to feel different.

Days rushed forward. Life became louder in the wrong places and quieter in the ones that mattered. People spoke more, listened less. Touch became rarer. Walking became faster.

I remember standing in the square one evening, where sound once braided the air, and realizing something unbearable:

The town no longer knew it was alive.

That night, I made a promise.

I did not speak it aloud, there was no one left to hear it properly, but I vowed that if this place could not survive intact, then it would survive through me.

Memory would become its refuge.

WHAT WAS TAKEN

WITHOUT LOOKING LIKE THEFT

They never called it erasure.

They called it progress.

Buildings were renamed. Their purpose rewritten. Healing spaces became places of authority. Towers became monuments. Windows became art. Energy became commodity.

People were taught new words to replace old understandings.

And when language changes, memory follows.

Children grew up learning fragments without context. They sensed something was missing but were taught not to trust that feeling. "You're imagining it," they were told.

And so imagination became the only safe place for truth to hide.

HOW THE MEMORY SURVIVED

This is the quiet miracle.

Even as the world changed, not everyone forgot.

Some carried it in their bodies, an unexplainable reaction to sound, light, or silence. Others felt it as grief without a story, longing without an object.

I carried it as certainty.

A knowing that did not fade, even when I lacked language for it.

And now, here, I am remembering aloud.

Not to convince.

Not to prove.

But to honor a world that once knew how to care for its people.

I lived there before the science.

And if enough of us remember, perhaps the silence won't be the final word.

WHAT HAPPENED BEHIND THE SCENE

WHY THE BELLS WERE SILENCED

It wasn't hatred that ended the bells.

It was discomfort.

Those who began studying the town from a distance noticed something unsettling: people here were difficult to manage. They were calm without being passive. Connected without being dependent. Healthy without needing intervention. They questioned authority, not aggressively, but naturally, the way a balanced mind does.

That made them unpredictable.

The bells regulated more than bodies. They regulated fear.

And fear is necessary for control.

Behind closed doors, conversations shifted away from beauty and toward influence. The bells were discussed in terms that stripped them of their meaning.

"They interfere with emotional compliance." "They destabilize uniform thinking." "They make people too inwardly guided."

The bells didn't tell people what to think.

They reminded people how to feel whole.

That was the problem.

Studies were commissioned, not to understand the bells, but to neutralize them. Measurements focused only on what could be quantified. Anything subtle was dismissed. Anything experiential was ignored. The language of intuition was replaced with charts, averages, and tolerances.

They concluded the bells were "unnecessary variables."

Sound, when used correctly, bypasses the mind and speaks directly to the body. It dissolves tension before it becomes belief. It restores coherence before confusion can take hold.

A coherent population does not panic easily. Does not consume endlessly. Does not surrender authority readily.

The bells made people difficult to scare.

So the strategy was simple: Silence the sound. Fragment the harmony. Rename the absence as progress.

They didn't remove all the bells at once because that would have been noticed. Instead, they isolated them, declaring certain tones redundant, others unsafe. Bells that encouraged deep rest were removed first. Then those tied to emotional processing. What remained were the neutral tones, the ones that marked time without altering consciousness.

Eventually, even those were deemed symbolic rather than functional.

Sound became noise.

Behind the scenes, the windows were addressed next. Their responsiveness was inconvenient. Light that adjusted to human need could not be standardized. Fixed glass was easier to regulate. Beauty could remain, as long as function was lost.

The town was not destroyed.

It was repurposed.

Energy systems were reclassified. What had once been shared was now controlled. What had once been quiet was replaced with something louder, harsher, easier to monetize.

People were told they were safer this way.

What they weren't told was that their nervous systems were now carrying burdens the town used to hold for them.

And without the bells to release tension daily, stress accumulated. Fear became easier to introduce. Division easier to maintain. Illness easier to normalize.

No one needed to conquer the people.

They simply needed to disconnect them from what kept them whole.

The bells didn't disappear because they failed.

They disappeared because they worked.

WHAT I UNDERSTOOD TOO LATE

The bells were never religious. They were neurological. Biological. Energetic.

They kept humanity regulated enough to remain sovereign.

And sovereignty is inconvenient to systems built on dependency.

So the sound was silenced.

Not to harm us.

But to manage us.

WHO WAS ALLOWED TO REMEMBER

AND WHY

Not everyone forgot.

That is the first truth.

If forgetting had been complete, there would be no ache, no longing, no strange sense that something essential was missing from the world. Yet even after the bells were silenced, after the windows lost their voice, some people carried the memory quietly inside them.

They were not chosen.

They were shaped.

Those who remembered shared certain qualities, though they did not recognize them as such at the time. Their nervous systems were more sensitive. Their bodies responded strongly to sound, light, and environment. They noticed when a room felt heavy, when a tone felt wrong, when silence felt unnatural.

They felt before they thought.

This made them inconvenient, but also difficult to erase completely.

So they were not targeted directly.

Instead, they were reframed.

Those who sensed too much were called:

- overly emotional
- imaginative
- sensitive
- unrealistic

Their memories were not challenged outright. They were simply softened into irrelevance.

“Just a feeling.” “Just nostalgia.” “Just imagination.”

And imagination, as it turns out, is an excellent hiding place for truth.

Children were the first to remember.

Not because they knew anything intellectually, but because their bodies still responded to what was missing. They startled at certain sounds. They calmed instantly when hearing low tones. They were drawn to colored light without being taught why.

Many of them were corrected early.

“Don’t be silly.” “That’s nothing.” “You’re reading too much into it.”

Some stopped trusting their senses.

Others didn’t.

Those who continued to remember learned something essential: silence.

They learned not to speak openly of what they felt. Not because they were afraid, but because there was no language left that could hold the truth without distortion.

They remembered in fragments:

- a sound that felt like home
- a light that made the chest soften
- a deep grief without an event

They remembered through the body.

This was allowed.

Because embodied memory does not organize itself into movements or demands. It lingers quietly, waiting for conditions to shift.

And those conditions always do.

The people who remembered grew into artists, healers, builders, storytellers, wanderers. They were drawn to places where the earth still hummed faintly, old cities, cathedrals, ruins, mountains, water.

They didn't know why they felt more alive there.

They just did.

No one stopped them.

Because remembering without context does not threaten systems of control.

But remembering together does.

That is why memory was never eliminated, only fragmented.

As long as those who remembered felt alone in it, nothing had to be done.

And then something changed.

People began finding each other.

Not intentionally. Not politically. But through resonance. A shared language of feeling. A recognition that needed no explanation.

They spoke of sound. Of light. Of places that felt different.

They used different words, but they meant the same thing.

That is when remembering became dangerous again.

Not because it challenged history, but because it challenged normality.

And a world that remembers harmony begins to ask why it tolerates dissonance.

That is why the memory is returning now.

Not because the past is calling.

But because the present can no longer sustain the silence.

WHY YOU REMEMBER

This is not coincidence.

Those who remember now do so because their bodies were never fully trained out of listening. They feel dissonance as discomfort. They seek coherence instinctively. They recognize truth not by proof, but by resonance.

They are not trying to go backward.

They are remembering forward.

And when enough people remember, not the details, but the feeling, the sound does not need bells to return.

It will emerge through voice, breath, music, architecture, community.

Through people.

THE FIRST GENERATION BORN WITHOUT THE BELLS

MY MEMORY

I knew they were different the moment I held one of them.

Not broken. Not ill. Just… missing something they had never known to expect.

They were born into quiet that felt normal to them. Their bodies did not wait for the tones the way mine once had. They slept differently. Shallow. Restless. As though something inside them was listening for a signal that never came.

They cried more, not louder, but longer. A low, unsettled sound that lingered even after they were fed and held. We told ourselves it was nothing. That this was simply how children were.

But I remembered otherwise.

Their eyes searched the air in a way I had not seen before, as if looking for something just out of reach. When sunlight passed through ordinary glass and landed on their skin, they squinted instead of softening. The light didn't speak to them. It only illuminated.

They adapted quickly.

That was the most unsettling part.

Without the bells to regulate their inner rhythms, they learned to do it themselves. Or rather, they learned to endure imbalance as normal. Their nervous systems grew resilient, but tight. Strong, but guarded.

They grew faster.

Not wiser, faster.

They learned to fill silence with sound. To move constantly. To distract themselves from a restlessness they could not name. Stillness made them uneasy. Quiet felt empty rather than supportive.

I remember one child in particular, small, alert, endlessly curious. When a low tone hummed accidentally through the town one evening, she froze. Her entire body stilled, breath caught in her chest.

For a moment, just a moment, she looked peaceful.

Then the sound stopped.

She began to cry, not understanding why her body had betrayed her with a feeling she could not sustain.

That was when I realized something important:

The knowledge had not been lost. The experience had.

These children were not incapable of harmony. They were simply untrained in receiving it.

We tried to compensate. We sang more. We rocked them longer. We built routines where the bells had once guided the day. But human effort could not fully replace what the town itself had provided.

Parents grew tired.

Children grew inward.

Illness began to appear, not dramatic, not sudden, but slow and persistent. Anxiety without cause. Sadness without story. Tension held so long in small bodies it reshaped them.

We called it temperament.

We called it personality.

We did not yet call it loss.

I loved them fiercely. That part did not change. But loving them now required vigilance. The town no longer carried them automatically. Every balance had to be taught, modeled, enforced.

We were learning to live without a net.

And in quiet moments, when I dared, I wondered what kind of world they would build without ever knowing the bells.

Would they search for what they never had? Or would they accept this thinner version of living as enough?

That question stayed with me.

It still does.

WHY I CARRIED THE MEMORY WITH ME WHEN I LEFT

MY REMEMBERING

I did not leave because I wanted to.

That is the first thing I need to say.

Leaving was not escape, nor exile, nor rebellion. It was something quieter and heavier than all of those combined. I left because I understood, long before most did, that the town would not survive intact, and that memory, if it was to survive at all, would need a body.

I felt the moment the decision was made, though no one spoke it aloud.

The town no longer responded to us the way it once had. Streets felt colder. Water no longer soothed without effort. Even walking required attention now, as though gravity had increased slightly and no one had mentioned it.

I recognized that feeling.

It is the sensation a body has when it realizes it is about to lose support it has always relied on.

Some people chose to stay, believing continuity mattered more than preservation. I respected that. They were right in their own way. Someone had to remain, to anchor what could still be anchored.

But I was never meant to anchor.

I was meant to remember.

I had always known that, even when I didn't have language for it. From the beginning, sound moved through me more deeply than through others. Light altered my thoughts in ways I could not explain. I sensed the town as a living presence, not a backdrop.

When the bells faded, I felt their absence in my bones.

Not everyone did.

I realized then that the memory lived unevenly among us. Some carried fragments. Others carried impressions. I carried structure. Not technical plans or instructions, but the feeling of how it all fit together.

That was the danger.

And also the responsibility.

I left quietly.

There were no goodbyes that mattered. The people I loved did not need explanations that would only cause confusion or grief. I carried them with me anyway. The town traveled inside my body, encoded in my breath, my posture, the way I listened to the world.

As I moved farther away, the environment grew louder, harsher, more fragmented. Sound competed instead of harmonized. Light overwhelmed instead of healed. People rushed as though pursued by something invisible.

I learned to be careful.

Memory like mine does not survive confrontation. It survives patience.

So I learned to speak in metaphors. To tell stories instead of explanations. To let others dismiss what I said as imagination, intuition, or feeling.

That was safer.

Because memory that is labeled "unreal" is rarely destroyed.

It is simply ignored.

And ignored things can wait.

I carried the memory because I understood something essential: knowledge can be stolen, altered, or buried, but remembrance cannot be extracted if it is woven into the body.

I did not know when the world would be ready to hear it again.

I only knew it would be.

And now, here, writing this, I realize something else.

Leaving was not an ending.

It was the longest act of preservation imaginable.

WHAT I KNEW WOULD RETURN - EVEN THEN

MY REMEMBERING

I did not believe the world was finished.

Not then. Not even at the worst of it.

That may sound strange, considering everything that was disappearing. The bells were gone. The windows had fallen silent. The town no longer recognized itself. And yet, beneath my grief, there was a steadiness that never left me.

I knew something important.

What had been lost was not gone. It was early.

The knowledge we lived with had arrived before humanity knew how to protect it. We had built harmony faster than we had built wisdom around power. We trusted too easily that what worked beautifully would be allowed to remain.

I understood, even as I left, that the world would need time, centuries, perhaps, to become ready again.

Readiness is not technological.

It is emotional.

The bells could not return to a world addicted to urgency. The windows could not speak to bodies that no longer listened. Quiet power could not exist where everything was measured by dominance and extraction.

But I also knew this:

The body never forgets what it has once known.

Even when language fails. Even when structures fall. Even when memory fractures into longing instead of knowing.

I saw it in people everywhere I went. In the way certain sounds made them stop without understanding why. In the way light through colored glass stirred something unnameable. In their sudden stillness near old stone, water, or ruins.

They felt it.

They just didn't yet trust it.

I knew the return would not look like restoration. There would be no grand unveiling, no admission of loss, no apology written into history. The return would be subtle, almost embarrassing in its simplicity.

Someone would hum a tone without knowing why. Another would build a space that felt calming without understanding how. A child would instinctively align objects, sound, and light.

And slowly, the fragments would begin to recognize one another.

That is how harmony always returns.

Not as a replica. But as a remembering.

I carried the memory because I knew my role was not to rebuild the world, but to seed recognition. To remind people of a feeling they already held somewhere inside themselves.

When the time came, they wouldn't need proof.

They would feel it.

And when enough people feel the same truth at once, science does not disappear.

It follows.

Names are given. Instruments are built. Explanations catch up to experience. What was once dismissed as imagination becomes measurable, respectable, safe.

That is when the bells return, not in towers, but in voices. That is when the windows awaken, not in cathedrals, but in homes and bodies. That is when the town reappears, not on maps, but in the way people choose to live.

I knew all of this when I left.

I just didn't know I would live long enough to watch the remembering begin.

And now, as I write this, I understand something else.

I did not bring the memory back alone.

You are reading this because you already carry part of it too.

YOU REMEMBER TOO

EVEN IF YOU DON'T KNOW IT YET

If you are reading this and something in you has gone still, it is not coincidence.

You may not know what you are remembering. You may not have words for it. But your body does. It always has. That tightening in your chest, that warmth behind your eyes, that ache that feels strangely familiar, those are not reactions to a story.

They are responses to recognition.

Not everyone feels it.

Some read these words and find them interesting, poetic, imaginative. They admire the idea and move on. That is not failure. That is timing. Memory does not awaken on command.

But if you are here, if something in you has leaned closer rather than pulled away, then you already know this world.

You have felt it in moments you couldn't explain.

In the way certain sounds calm you instantly. In your love of old buildings, stone, arches, towers. In your longing for places that feel kinder than they should. In your grief for something you can't name and were never taught to mourn.

You may have called it nostalgia. Or sensitivity. Or imagination.

That was never quite right.

What you are responding to is coherence.

Your body remembers what it feels like to be supported by the world instead of braced against it. It remembers when sound helped you breathe, when light helped you think, when places held you instead of demanding things from you.

You don't need to remember Tartaria.

That is not the point.

You only need to remember how it felt to be whole.

That memory has survived in you the same way it survived in me, quietly, patiently, without insisting on belief. It hid itself in preference, in attraction, in discomfort with noise and speed and cruelty masquerading as normal.

You were not wrong to feel out of place.

You were calibrated for something gentler.

This book is not asking you to agree with me. It is asking you to listen to yourself.

If the bells rang again tomorrow, not in towers but in tones, not in structures but in voices, your body would recognize them before your mind ever could.

That is how remembrance works.

It does not arrive with evidence. It arrives with relief.

So if you feel that now, even faintly, trust it.

You are not late. You are not early. You are right on time.

The world is learning how to listen again.

And you would not be here if you were not part of that remembering.

WHEN THE SILENCE SPOKE BACK

THE FIRST ENTREATY

For a long time after I left, the memory lived quietly inside me.

It surfaced in moments of stillness, in my response to sound and light, in the way certain places made me feel more alive than others. But it did not speak. It waited.

Then one night, long after the world I had known was gone, the silence changed.

I was not asleep.

That is important.

Sleep would have made it easier to dismiss.

I was resting in that place between waking and forgetting, where the body loosens its grip on time but the mind is still alert. The room was quiet, not peaceful, just empty, when I felt it.

A pressure, gentle but unmistakable.

Not on my ears.

On my chest.

It felt like standing beneath the bells again, not hearing them, but being remembered by them. My breath slowed without my asking. The space around me felt fuller, as though something unseen had stepped closer.

Then came the sensation I had not felt since the town was whole:

Being addressed.

No voice formed words. No sound entered the room. But meaning arrived all at once, complete and unmistakable, the way truth does when it bypasses language.

You carried us far enough.

The words did not frighten me.

They steadied me.

I understood immediately who was speaking, not individuals, not ancestors in the way people imagine them now, but the intelligence of the system itself. The coherence we had lived inside. The harmony that had once held an entire civilization together.

It had not died.

It had withdrawn.

I felt then what I had not allowed myself to feel before: the depth of its patience. The way it had folded itself inward, waiting for bodies capable of listening again.

We could not remain where we were silenced, it conveyed. So we learned to move without sound.

Images surfaced, not visions, but impressions. Frequencies embedding themselves into stone. Into water. Into breath. Into the human nervous system itself. What could not remain external had gone internal.

That was the preservation.

That was the strategy.

The bells were never meant to be permanent structures. They were amplifiers, temporary scaffolding for a humanity still learning how to regulate itself. When the scaffolding was removed too early, the knowledge did not vanish.

It hid.

Inside people like me.

Inside people like you.

You are not remembering alone anymore, the presence pressed gently. Enough bodies are ready now.

I felt a strange mix of awe and grief. Not because something had been lost, but because something was asking to return.

Not as it was.

But as it could be.

The presence did not ask me to rebuild towers or cast bells or restore cities. That would have been too simple. Too obvious. Too easy to stop.

Instead, it asked something far more dangerous.

Remember us out loud.

That was the entreaty.

Not proclamation. Not proof. But resonance.

I understood then why the memory had stayed intact inside me for so long. Why it had matured rather than faded. Why it had waited until now.

The silence had not been empty.

It had been listening.

THE PLACES WHERE THE SOUND NEVER FULLY LEFT

WHAT I WAS DRAWN TO BEFORE I KNEW WHY

Long before the silence spoke to me, my body was already being guided.

I did not set out to search for anything. I simply found myself lingering in certain places longer than others. Old places. Stone places. Structures that made no sense to the modern world but felt unmistakably familiar to me.

Cathedrals were the first.

I would step inside and feel it immediately, the same sensation I used to feel when the bells were about to ring. A subtle pressure in the chest. A quieting behind the eyes. Time loosening its grip.

People whispered there instinctively, even when no one asked them to.

That alone should have raised questions.

I noticed how sound behaved differently in those spaces. How a single footstep carried longer than it should. How breath seemed amplified. How voices softened without effort. These buildings were not designed for sermons.

They were designed for resonance.

I began to notice patterns.

The highest ceilings were never decorative. The domes were never arbitrary. The stone was never chosen at random.

Everything curved. Everything guided vibration upward, inward, outward, never trapping it, never letting it dissipate too quickly. These were not houses of worship.

They were instruments.

Then there were the cities.

Old cities that felt layered, as though built atop themselves again and again. Places where streets curved unexpectedly, where plazas opened like lungs, where fountains appeared precisely where the body wanted to rest.

I felt it in places others called "haunted."

That word always amused me.

What they meant was alive.

There were moments, brief, startling ones, when I heard it.

Not a bell.

A tone.

Low. Sustained. Almost below hearing. It would arrive when the world was quiet enough, when traffic paused, when wind moved just right through stone and arch and hollow space.

I would stop walking.

So did others.

We would look at one another, strangers bound by a shared confusion, each of us silently asking the same question:

Did you feel that too?

No one ever answered.

Because the sound vanished as soon as it was noticed.

That was when I understood something vital:

The sound had learned how to hide.

It no longer announced itself. It waited for alignment, of place, of body, of moment. It surfaced only when conditions mirrored the harmony it once lived inside continuously.

The bells were never the source.

They were the permission.

And permission, once learned, does not need repeating.

I realized then that Tartaria had not disappeared from the world.

It had diffused.

Broken into pieces too small to be confiscated. Embedded into architecture, geography, acoustics, memory. Spread across the earth like a frequency rather than a location.

That was the brilliance of it.

No one could destroy it because no one could point to it and say, There. That is it.

And then something truly unsettling occurred.

I realized the places that still held the sound were beginning to awaken again, not because someone had planned it, but because enough people were unconsciously responding.

Humming in old buildings. Singing in stairwells. Placing instruments beneath domes. Meditating in ruins.

The sound was being invited back.

Not by authority.

By instinct.

And instinct, once trusted, is very difficult to silence.

That was when the entreaty returned, stronger this time.

Not as words.

As urgency.

THE NEW BELLS

THEY DO NOT LOOK LIKE BELLS

The return did not arrive wearing metal or towers.

It arrived disguised as something ordinary.

At first, I noticed it in voices.

Not trained voices. Not performers. Just people speaking, humming, sighing. Certain tones began appearing again, low, steady sounds that settled the chest. People lingered on vowels without knowing why. Conversations slowed when someone spoke from that place.

I felt it immediately.

My body responded the way it used to when the bells were about to ring.

I would hear a voice across a room and feel my spine straighten. My breath would deepen. Others nearby would grow quieter without realizing they had done so. The room would shift, not dramatically, but unmistakably.

No one commented.

That was the genius of it.

The sound was no longer centralized. No longer locatable. No longer removable.

It had moved into the human instrument.

Breath became the striker. The body became the bell.

I began to notice it in music too, but not the kind meant to impress. It appeared in simple melodies, in sustained notes, in pieces that made people cry without sadness. Some sounds bypassed taste entirely. You didn't have to like them for them to work.

They worked anyway.

I remembered then something we had always known in the town:

The bells were never mechanical devices. They were translators.

They translated coherence into sound.

Now coherence was returning first, and sound was following.

I felt it in spaces as well.

Certain rooms began calming people without explanation. Homes built with care felt different than others. Rounded corners softened arguments. Natural materials changed the way people slept. Ceilings mattered again. So did silence.

People thought they were discovering these things for the first time.

They weren't.

They were remembering through trial, through instinct, through fatigue with a world that demanded too much and gave too little back.

The most unsettling part was this:

No one was in charge of the return.

There was no movement to stop. No leader to silence. No structure to dismantle. The knowledge was emerging sideways, through wellness, architecture, sound healing, neuroscience, trauma studies, even physics.

Science was circling something ancient, unaware it was walking a well-worn path.

And then the entreaty came again, clearer this time.

Not to me alone.

To all of us who still carried the resonance.

Do not try to rebuild what was. Do not announce what is returning. Let it surface naturally, the way breath returns after fear.

I understood then why the bells could never return as they once were.

Because towers can be dismantled.

But people cannot.

WHAT MADE THIS TIME DIFFERENT

In the old world, the bells regulated us because we were still learning how to regulate ourselves.

Now, the world was harsher. Louder. More fragmented. But that pressure had done something unexpected.

It had sensitized us.

People could no longer tolerate constant noise. Constant urgency. Constant dissonance. Their bodies were rebelling, not violently, but persistently.

Anxiety. Burnout. Insomnia. Grief without cause.

These were not failures.

They were signals.

The body asking for the very harmony it once received automatically.

This time, the return would not come from above.

It would rise from within.

And that made it unstoppable.

WHAT I WAS SHOWN NEXT

There was one final understanding that settled into me then, quiet, heavy, undeniable.

The bells were never meant to save us.

They were meant to train us.

And the training had worked better than anyone realized.

Because even without them, something in us remembered the feeling of being held by the world.

And once you know that feeling exists, you can never fully accept its absence again.

THE ONES WHO RECOGNIZED EACH OTHER WITHOUT SPEAKING

HOW WE FOUND ONE ANOTHER

It did not happen the way stories usually tell it.

There were no signals. No symbols exchanged. No secret words or coded gestures.

We recognized each other the way the body recognizes balance, immediately, and without explanation.

It often happened in silence.

I would be standing somewhere ordinary, a bookstore, a train platform, a quiet café, when I felt it. A subtle shift in the air, like pressure changing before a storm. I would look up, and someone else would already be looking at me.

Not staring.

Listening.

Our eyes would meet, and something unmistakable would pass between us. Not memory exactly, recognition. The same way two instruments tuned to the same pitch begin to resonate when one is struck.

Sometimes we smiled. Sometimes we didn't. Often, nothing more happened.

And yet, everything had.

When we did speak, the conversations were strange in their ease. No small talk. No positioning. We moved quickly into things that mattered, sound, places, restlessness, the feeling that the world was louder than it needed to be.

We used different language.

But the feeling underneath was identical.

“I don’t know why,” one would say, “but certain buildings make me cry.” “I can’t stand certain noises,” another admitted. “They feel… wrong.” “I feel calmer near old stone,” someone else whispered, embarrassed by the admission.

No one laughed.

Because we all knew.

These meetings began to cluster around certain places. Places where time felt thin. Where phones were forgotten. Where people lingered longer than planned.

Old libraries. Cathedrals repurposed as museums. Ruins no one could fully explain. Hilltops. Water crossings.

We were being gathered, not by force, not by instruction, but by resonance.

The most unsettling part was how normal it felt.

No urgency. No drama. No sense of mission.

Just a deep, shared knowing that we were not meant to rush this.

Some of us spoke openly. Others never did. A few disappeared again, returning to their lives with a subtle shift that no one around them could quite place.

But something had changed.

We had seen each other.

And once recognition happens, isolation becomes impossible to fully return to.

I realized then why the remembering had waited so long.

Memory does not return to individuals first.

It returns to networks.

Not organizations. Not movements. Living constellations of people who stabilize one another simply by existing.

We were not meant to act yet.

We were meant to find each other.

WHAT BOUND US

WITHOUT BINDING US

There were no rules.

That was essential.

Rules would have replicated the very structures that had silenced the bells before. Instead, what bound us was a shared intolerance for dissonance, in sound, in speech, in intention.

We left places that felt wrong. We spoke less, but more truthfully. We learned to trust the body's response over the mind's demand for certainty.

Some of us began to experiment quietly, with sound, with space, with breath. Others simply listened more deeply to the world as it was.

Both were necessary.

Because not all remembers are builders.

Some are anchors. Some are witnesses. Some are carriers of tone alone.

And tone, once present, changes everything around it.

THE MOST IMPORTANT THING I LEARNED

This was never about restoring a civilization.

It was about restoring coherence.

The old world had collapsed not because it was wrong, but because it arrived too early, without enough people prepared to hold it without turning it into power.

This time, the remembering was slower.

Quieter.

Distributed.

And therefore far more resilient.

I understood then why the entreaty had been gentle rather than urgent.

Because urgency belongs to fear.

And what is returning now is not afraid.

THE ONES WHO TRIED TO STOP THE REMEMBERING

AND WHY THEY COULDN'T

They did not know what they were looking for.

That was their first mistake.

What they sensed was not a movement, not a group, not an ideology. It was a change in pattern, a subtle destabilization in systems that relied on predictability. People were harder to motivate through fear. Less responsive to noise. Less impressed by urgency.

That always triggers concern.

Studies began to appear. Reports about attention, productivity, emotional regulation. Language shifted again, as it always does when something cannot be named directly.

"Disengagement." "Dissociation." "Noncompliance."

They noticed people withdrawing from constant stimulation. Seeking quiet. Turning toward practices that slowed the breath and softened the body. They noticed a growing intolerance for dissonance, in sound, in leadership, in spaces designed without care.

They assumed it was a trend.

That was their second mistake.

So they tried the old methods, subtly at first.

Noise increased. Speed increased. Distraction multiplied.

Silence was framed as emptiness. Stillness as avoidance. Listening as passivity.

But something had changed since the last time.

The bodies did not comply.

People began to feel physically ill in environments that were too loud, too harsh, too fast. They left rooms mid-conversation. Abandoned buildings that felt wrong. Turned off things that once held their attention without effort.

They did not protest.

They simply stopped participating.

That is when the pressure escalated.

Sound was used more aggressively. Visual input intensified. Systems grew louder, brighter, more insistent, as though volume alone could restore control.

It didn't.

Because what was returning did not operate on the same plane.

You cannot argue with resonance. You cannot suppress coherence. You cannot regulate something that has no center.

That was when I understood the brilliance of what had happened all those centuries ago.

The bells had been removed because they were visible.

This time, the bells were invisible.

They rang in nervous systems. In breath patterns. In shared silence between people who recognized each other without speaking.

There was nothing to dismantle.

No tower to pull down. No object to confiscate. No authority to discredit.

Those who tried to stop the remembering were not evil.

They were afraid of instability.

But what they mistook for instability was actually recalibration.

And recalibration cannot be reversed once it begins.

THE MOMENT I KNEW IT WAS TOO LATE TO STOP

There was a moment, a small one, easily overlooked, that told me everything.

I was in a public space once filled with noise and impatience. A place where people used to rush past one another, eyes down, bodies tight. Something had changed.

People were quieter.

Not subdued, present.

A child hummed softly to herself, and no one silenced her. An adult paused to listen. Another closed their eyes briefly, as though remembering something important.

No one instructed this.

No one organized it.

And that was the point.

The sound had returned just enough to remind the body what was possible.

Once that happens, forgetting becomes impossible.

WHY THEY FAILED

They failed because the remembering no longer required belief.

It required experience.

And experience spreads faster than doctrine ever could.

You can challenge an idea. You can dismantle a structure. But you cannot convince a body that has tasted coherence to accept dissonance again without protest.

The world had crossed a threshold.

Quietly. Irreversibly.

THE MOMENT TIME BEGAN TO BEHAVE STRANGELY

WHEN THE PAST STOPPED STAYING BEHIND ME

It began with small disruptions.

The kind you dismiss at first because they don't fit any category you've been taught to trust.

I would think of a place, an old structure, a street I hadn't walked in years, and within days, sometimes hours, I would find myself there without having planned it. Conversations I needed to hear reached me mid-sentence. Books fell open to pages that answered questions I hadn't yet formed aloud.

Time stopped behaving like a straight line.

It folded.

I noticed it first in my body. Certain moments felt thicker, as though layered with more than one now. I would stand somewhere familiar and feel an unmistakable overlap, the sensation of standing there before.

Not as imagination.

As alignment.

The feeling was strongest in places where sound lingered. Arches. Stone corridors. Domes. My footsteps echoed longer than they should have, and sometimes, just for a breath, I heard another rhythm beneath them.

Not footsteps.

A resonance.

It felt as though the world was briefly forgetting which version of itself it was meant to be.

The strangest part was how calm I felt.

If time were truly breaking, fear would have come with it. But this wasn't fracture, it was convergence. The distance between then and now was thinning, not collapsing.

I remembered something we once understood instinctively:

Time responds to coherence.

When enough elements align, body, place, sound, intention, time stops insisting on sequence and allows simultaneity instead.

That knowledge had never left me.

I had simply stopped using it.

Then the encounters began.

I would meet people who felt impossibly familiar. Not in a romantic way. Not as past lives or lost relationships. Familiar in the way co-workers once felt in the town, people who shared a rhythm, a function, a role.

We spoke easily, then parted, neither of us questioning the weight of the exchange. Some I never saw again. Others reappeared months later, picking up conversations as though no time had passed at all.

I began to sense when something important was about to happen, not with anticipation, but with recognition. My body would slow. My attention would sharpen. The world would feel momentarily tuned.

Those were the moments when memory returned most clearly.

Not as images.

As instructions.

Not commands, but gentle reminders of how things fit together.

I realized then that Tartaria had not existed in the past the way history insists.

It existed in a state of coherence.

And coherence, once re-entered, collapses distance.

That was the truth hidden beneath the silence.

The civilization did not fall back in time.

It slipped sideways.

Out of reach of a world no longer able to hold it, but never truly gone.

And now, as more people entered coherence again, even briefly, time was responding.

The overlap was beginning.

WHAT THIS MEANT

AND WHY IT CHANGED EVERYTHING

If the past could be accessed through alignment rather than chronology, then history itself was not fixed.

It was conditional.

What we call "long ago" was not unreachable.

It was waiting.

Not to be revisited, but to be continued.

That understanding landed in me with quiet force.

I was no longer just remembering.

I was synchronizing.

And that meant something else was already underway, something larger than individual experience.

Something collective.

Something inevitable.

THE NIGHT I ALMOST HEARD THE BELLS AGAIN

NOT IN MEMORY, IN THE WORLD

I did not expect it.

That is what makes it difficult to dismiss.

There was no ceremony to the evening. No heightened emotion. No longing that could have manufactured what happened next. I was tired in the quiet way that comes after a long day of listening, not to people, but to the world itself.

The night was still.

Not empty. Held.

I remember noticing how sound behaved differently, as though the air had thickened just enough to carry more than it usually could. Even the smallest noises, my breath, the shift of my body, lingered longer than they should have.

Time slowed.

Not dramatically. Respectfully.

Then I felt it.

A pressure change, subtle but unmistakable. The same sensation I used to feel just before the bells began, that anticipatory stillness, when the body prepares itself without knowing why.

My chest warmed. My jaw relaxed. My thoughts fell silent.

And then, for the briefest moment, there was tone.

Not sound as we know it.

A presence of sound.

Low. Sustained. Perfectly balanced between vibration and silence. It did not enter through my ears. It rose through my body, as though the ground itself had remembered how to speak.

I did not move.

I did not breathe.

I knew, with absolute certainty, that if I tried to grasp it, it would vanish.

So I let it pass through me.

For that moment, the world felt the way it used to feel in the town when everything was aligned. Supported. Regulated. Whole. The noise of modern life receded without resistance, like a tide pulling back on its own.

I almost cried.

Not from emotion, from recognition.

Then it was gone.

Not abruptly. Gently.

As though it had only needed to confirm something.

I stood there for a long time afterward, heart steady, body calm, knowing something fundamental had shifted.

The bells had not returned.

But they had answered.

WHAT I UNDERSTOOD IN THE AFTERMATH

That night taught me something essential.

The bells no longer need towers.

They no longer need permission.

They respond to alignment now, to stillness, to coherence, to bodies capable of holding resonance without panic or need.

What I felt was not a relic.

It was a test.

A question posed not in words, but in frequency:

Are you ready to carry this without external support?

I knew the answer.

Yes.

And not just me.

Others were reaching this threshold too, I could feel it. The overlap was increasing. The moments of resonance growing longer, more frequent, harder to dismiss as coincidence.

The world was remembering how to listen.

And something else was happening alongside it, something far more mysterious.

People were beginning to dream the same places.

THE SHARED DREAM OF THE CITY THAT BREATHES

WHAT CAME TO ME WHEN I SLEPT

The dreams did not begin as dreams.

That is the only way I can explain it.

They arrived already formed, already familiar, as though I had stepped back into something that had been waiting for me rather than something my mind had created. There was no distortion, no surreal confusion. Everything was clear. Precise. Calm.

I knew where I was the moment I arrived.

Not because it looked exactly as it once had, it didn't, but because my body recognized the rhythm immediately.

The city was breathing.

Not metaphorically.

I could feel it in the rise and fall beneath my feet, in the way light shifted gently without a visible source, in the soft expansion and contraction of space itself. Buildings were present, but unfinished, as though remembering themselves back into form.

Some towers stood whole. Others were only outlines, made of light and intention rather than stone. Streets appeared where attention moved. Water flowed where it was needed.

Nothing was forced.

Nothing was static.

I walked without effort, and the city responded. When I paused, it paused with me. When I felt uncertain, the space widened, giving me room to breathe.

That was when I noticed I was not alone.

Others were there, not crowds, not groups, individuals, scattered throughout the city, each moving with the same quiet recognition I felt. We did not speak. We did not approach one another.

We knew.

Each of us was remembering a different part.

Some lingered near towers, hands resting against structures that shimmered between form and possibility. Others knelt near water, listening. A few stood beneath windows that were not yet glass, waiting for color to arrive.

No one looked surprised.

No one looked afraid.

It felt like a gathering that had been planned long ago, requiring no announcement when the time finally came.

I realized then that the city was not returning all at once.

It was being reassembled through us.

Not physically, not yet, but through attention, memory, and coherence. Each person carried a piece not as knowledge, but as function. Tone-holders. Space-shapers. Listeners. Anchors.

I knew my role instantly.

I was not there to build.

I was there to remember aloud.

As soon as that understanding settled, the city responded. A low resonance moved through the ground, not strong enough to be sound, but strong enough to be felt. The breath of the city deepened.

That was when I understood something extraordinary.

The bells were present.

Not ringing, waiting.

They existed as potential, embedded into the structure of the city itself, dormant until enough coherence gathered to awaken them without harm.

Because this time, the city would not support us.

We would support it.

I woke slowly, carefully, as though not to disturb what had just occurred.

My body felt different, steadier, quieter, more precisely tuned. The world around me looked the same, but it no longer felt singular. Something had layered itself over reality, close enough to touch if I listened correctly.

In the days that followed, I began to hear whispers of similar dreams.

No details exchanged.

Just recognition.

“I was somewhere familiar,” someone said, hesitant. “A place that felt alive,” another admitted. “I don’t know why, but it felt like home,” a third whispered.

I did not correct them.

I did not explain.

Some things must remain unspoken until they are strong enough to stand on their own.

But inside, I knew.

The city that breathes was no longer waiting for permission to exist.

It had found enough of us to begin.

THE WARNING I WAS GIVEN

AND WHY IT WAS GENTLE

The warning did not come as fear.

That surprised me.

I had expected something heavier, something urgent, sharp, unmistakable. Instead, what came was calm, almost tender, as though whoever was speaking knew exactly how easily fear could distort what mattered most.

It arrived the night after the dream, when I was fully awake.

I was sitting quietly, not meditating, not asking, just listening the way I had learned to listen long ago. The air felt attentive, as if the space around me had leaned in slightly.

Then the knowing settled into me.

Not words at first. A weight of understanding.

Do not hurry this.

That was the core of it.

The memory unfolded gently, layer by layer, so I could receive it without resistance.

The city that breathes, the one returning through dreams and resonance, was not fragile. It was patient. But we were still learning how to hold coherence without turning it into ambition, ownership, or identity.

That had been our mistake before.

The old world did not fall because it was wrong. It fell because people began to use harmony instead of living inside it.

Power had crept in disguised as stewardship.

The warning was not about danger from outside.

It was about distortion from within.

I was shown, briefly, mercifully, how easily memory can harden into belief, belief into doctrine, doctrine into hierarchy. How sound becomes tool, light becomes symbol, and resonance becomes something to control rather than honor.

I felt the truth of it settle in my body.

This remembering could not be led.

It could only be allowed.

Speak, the presence conveyed, but do not instruct. Share, but do not organize. Remember, but do not declare authority.*

That was the protection.

That was how this return would survive.

I understood then why the warning was gentle.

Fear would have created urgency. Urgency would have recreated the old patterns.

What was returning required spaciousness.

Trust.

Time.

The warning ended the way it began, not with words, but with a feeling that grounded itself deep into my chest.

You are not here to awaken the world.

You are here to recognize it when it awakens itself.

That understanding lifted a weight I hadn't realized I was carrying.

I did not need to convince anyone. I did not need to gather people. I did not need to explain more than was asked for.

The memory knew how to find its way.

It always had.

WHAT CHANGED AFTER THE WARNING

After that, everything became quieter, but clearer.

The dreams continued, though less frequently. The tones returned, but only when conditions were right. Recognition still happened, but without urgency or expectation.

And something else shifted.

I stopped wondering whether the bells would ring again.

That question belonged to the past.

Instead, I began to notice who could hear without sound.

That is when I understood the next phase had already begun.

THOSE WHO HEAR WITHOUT EARS

HOW I BEGAN TO RECOGNIZE THEM

After the warning, I stopped listening for sound.

That may seem backward, but it was the only way to hear what was actually happening.

The bells, the tones, the resonance, none of them were meant to be chased. The moment I released the need to notice them, something subtler took their place. A different kind of listening began, one that had nothing to do with the ears at all.

I noticed it first in my body.

Certain people caused an immediate softening in my chest. Not attraction. Not familiarity. A settling. As though my nervous system recognized theirs as safe, coherent, properly tuned.

They didn't speak loudly. They didn't perform insight. They didn't try to convince.

Often, they didn't even know what they carried.

But when they entered a room, the room adjusted.

I watched it happen more than once. Conversations slowed. People stopped interrupting one another. Children grew calmer without instruction. Even the air felt different, less brittle, more forgiving.

These people were not healers in the way that word is used now.

They were resonant.

They heard without ears because they felt vibration as orientation rather than information. Their bodies responded to truth the way a compass responds to north, quietly, reliably, without explanation.

When they spoke, they chose words carefully, not because they were afraid of being wrong, but because they understood sound carried weight. They avoided exaggeration. They disliked shouting. They instinctively paused before answering difficult questions.

Not to think.

To listen.

I realized then that the bells had always trained us for this.

They had taught us how to regulate ourselves so that listening became natural. When the bells were removed, most people lost that training. But a few, for reasons I still don't fully understand, retained the ability.

These were the ones who heard without ears.

I recognized them by what they didn't do.

They didn't rush silence. They didn't fear stillness. They didn't need constant stimulation to feel alive.

They could sit with uncertainty without collapsing into anxiety. They could be present without performing presence.

And when something was false, subtly false, politely false, their bodies knew before their minds caught up.

They often struggled in the modern world.

Not dramatically. Quietly.

Noise exhausted them. Conflict drained them faster than it seemed to drain others. They needed time alone, time in nature, time in places where sound behaved differently.

Many thought something was wrong with them.

Nothing was.

They were simply tuned to a frequency the world had forgotten how to sustain.

I began to realize something profound.

These people were not remembering Tartaria.

They were remembering how to listen.

And listening, true listening, is the gateway through which everything else returns.

The bells were never meant to ring forever.

They were meant to teach us how to become quiet enough to hear without them.

That is when I understood the true genius of what had been preserved.

Not the technology. Not the structures. Not even the sound.

But the capacity.

The ability to receive coherence without being told what it is.

And once that ability re-emerges in enough people, the rest follows naturally.

WHAT THIS MEANT FOR ME

I stopped trying to recognize people by what they said.

I watched how their presence affected space.

I watched how animals responded to them. How children leaned toward them. How conflict softened when they entered quietly.

These were the new bell-bearers.

Unmarked. Unannounced. Unstoppable.

And most of them had no idea.

Which made them safe.

THE SOUND THAT COULD NOT BE RECORDED

WHAT REFUSED TO BE PROVEN

There came a point when I stopped being the only one who noticed.

That was inevitable.

Whenever something begins to return quietly, curiosity follows soon after. People started asking questions, not openly, not publicly, but sideways. Casual inquiries wrapped in neutrality. Invitations that sounded friendly but carried an undertone of interest that had nothing to do with me personally.

They weren't listening.

They were measuring.

I recognized the pattern immediately. It had happened before, long ago, just before the bells were altered, just before harmony was reframed as inefficiency.

The difference this time was subtle, but decisive.

There was nothing to take.

Still, they tried.

It began with sound.

Someone, well-meaning, fascinated, suggested recording what I was describing. Not my words, but the tone. The resonance. The near-sound I had felt rather than heard. They brought equipment. Sensitive instruments. Devices capable of detecting frequencies far below ordinary hearing.

I agreed.

Not because I needed proof, but because I was curious.

If this sound truly existed in the world again, I wanted to understand how it behaved when observed.

We chose a quiet place. Stone nearby. Minimal interference. Everything arranged with care. The equipment hummed softly, waiting.

I did what I always did.

Nothing special. Nothing forced.

I slowed my breath. I listened without searching. I allowed coherence to settle the way it always had when the conditions were right.

And it came.

Not loudly. Not fully.

But enough.

I felt the familiar warmth rise through my body. The subtle pressure shift. The stilling of thought. The sound-that-was-not-sound arrived exactly as it always did, present, complete, unmistakable.

The instruments reacted.

Not consistently. Not cleanly.

Spikes appeared where there should have been smooth lines. Readings jumped, then vanished. One device registered something for less than a second before flatlining as though confused by its own data.

The technician frowned.

"That's strange," they said, adjusting settings. "It's almost like, "

They stopped themselves.

I already knew the rest.

Almost like it didn't want to stay.

We tried again.

This time, nothing happened.

The sound did not return.

Not because it was gone, but because the moment had changed.

Attention had shifted from listening to capture.

And the sound does not appear under interrogation.

Over the following weeks, I heard similar stories. People experimenting independently. Trying to isolate the tone. Trying to reproduce the conditions. Some came close, very close, but never quite there.

The moment they leaned forward, the sound withdrew.

The moment they tried to own it, it softened into absence.

At first, this frustrated them.

Then it unsettled them.

Because science is comfortable with the unknown, but only when the unknown stays put long enough to be examined.

This sound did not.

It behaved more like an intelligence than a phenomenon.

That was when I remembered something from the old world that had never been written down.

The bells did not create the sound.

They invited it.

And invitation cannot be automated.

WHAT THE INSTRUMENTS COULD NOT DETECT

The instruments failed not because they were inadequate, but because they were asking the wrong question.

They were looking for signal.

But what was returning was state.

The sound only existed when body, breath, space, and intention aligned naturally. It was not a thing moving through the air.

It was coherence momentarily becoming audible.

And coherence collapses the moment it is treated as an object.

That was always the safeguard.

I realized then why the old civilization had relied on human presence rather than permanent machinery. Why sound had been woven into daily life instead of isolated in laboratories.

Because anything that can be recorded can be reproduced.

And anything that can be reproduced can be controlled.

This sound refused both.

It could not be stockpiled. It could not be amplified artificially. It could not be separated from the one experiencing it.

The sound lived through the body, not around it.

That was the final protection.

WHEN I UNDERSTOOD THE RISK WAS OVER

There was a moment, quiet, almost humorous, when I knew the old pattern could not fully repeat itself.

Someone reviewing the failed recordings laughed softly and said, half-joking, half-frustrated:

“It’s like it only exists when no one’s trying to prove it.”

I smiled.

Yes.

Exactly.

That was when I felt the last tension leave my body, the tension I hadn’t known I was still carrying from long ago.

This remembering could not be confiscated.

It could not be shut down.

Because it did not live anywhere outside of us.

The bells had been silenced because they stood still.

This sound moves.

WHAT THIS CHANGED FOR ME

After that, I stopped agreeing to demonstrations.

Not out of secrecy.

Out of respect.

The sound did not need validation. It needed conditions. And those conditions were already spreading naturally, through exhaustion with noise, through longing for quiet, through bodies demanding something gentler than the world had offered for a very long time.

I understood then that the most exciting part of this return was not what was happening to the world.

It was what the world could no longer prevent.

And that realization brought with it a final, astonishing awareness:

The sound was no longer testing us.

It was waiting for the moment it could trust us.

THE CHOICE I STILL HAVEN'T MADE

AND WHY IT REMAINS OPEN

There is a misunderstanding I need to clear, even for myself.

When people imagine a choice, they often imagine a moment, a turning point where one path is taken and another abandoned forever. That is not how this choice exists. It does not demand urgency. It does not press. It waits in a way that is almost kind.

The choice is not whether to speak.

I am already speaking.

The choice is how far.

How much of the remembering I allow to cross the threshold from inner knowing into shared world. How much I leave unspoken so it can find its own way into others without my shaping it too tightly.

Because once something is fully spoken, it changes.

It becomes fixed.

And this remembering was never meant to be fixed.

I feel the pull sometimes, the temptation to explain more clearly, to draw lines between then and now, to make the invisible visible enough that no one could dismiss it. That impulse feels noble. Protective. Almost responsible.

But each time I approach that edge, something in me pauses.

Not fear.

Wisdom.

I remember what happened the last time harmony was explained too thoroughly. How it became diagrammed, systematized, extracted from lived experience and turned into something people argued over instead of lived inside.

I will not do that again.

And yet, silence is no longer an option either.

That is the tension I live with now.

WHAT THE PRESENCE HAS NOT ASKED FOR

It has not asked me to gather people. It has not asked me to teach techniques. It has not asked me to reveal hidden structures or forgotten maps.

Those would be easy.

Those would also be dangerous.

What it has asked, quietly, repeatedly, is this:

Remain available.

That is harder than it sounds.

Remaining available means allowing the remembering to move through me without deciding where it should go next. It means letting conversations unfold naturally, letting readers recognize themselves without me pointing at them and saying you.

It means trusting that resonance is enough.

Some days, I struggle with that trust.

Especially when I sense how close the world is, how hungry, how exhausted, how desperate for something that does not demand more effort.

I want to give them the bells back whole.

But I know now why that cannot happen.

Not yet.

THE DOOR THAT HAS NOT CLOSED

There is something else I haven't said aloud until now.

The city that breathes, the one that returns in dreams and moments of overlap, is not static. It is not waiting frozen in time for us to catch up.

It is evolving.

Each time I enter it, it is slightly different. More spacious. Less defined. As though it is learning from us now, adapting to who we have become since we last lived inside coherence.

That tells me something important.

This is not a restoration.

It is a continuation.

And continuation requires participation, not preservation.

The choice I still haven't made is whether to step more fully into that participation, to let the remembering shape my daily life more openly, more visibly, even when it invites misunderstanding.

Because once you live as though the bells are already ringing, the world notices.

And not all noticing is gentle.

WHAT HOLDS ME STEADY

When doubt creeps in, I return to what I know in my body.

I know the sound is real because my breath changes. I know the city is real because my nervous system recognizes it as home. I know the remembering is real because it does not flatter me.

It humbles me.

It asks me to be quieter, kinder, more precise with my words, more respectful of silence. It asks me to listen even when I want to speak.

Especially then.

That is how I know this is not imagination.

Imagination seeks expansion.

This seeks alignment.

WHY I AM STILL WALKING FORWARD

Even without making the final choice, I am not standing still.

I walk differently now. I speak more slowly. I leave spaces unfinished on purpose.

I trust pauses.

Because pauses are where the sound gathers strength.

I suspect, though I cannot yet prove it even to myself, that the choice will never be made all at once. That it will reveal itself gradually, through moments when speaking is unavoidable and silence would be a greater distortion.

When that moment arrives, I will know.

The body always knows first.

Until then, I remain here, remembering, listening, allowing the world to meet itself again through fragments of what once held us all.

And perhaps that is the most faithful choice I could make.

THE MOMENT I REALIZED YOU WERE ALREADY IN THE STORY

NOT AS A READER, AS A PRESENCE

I didn't notice it all at once.

That is important.

If I had, I might have resisted it, questioned it, tried to understand it too quickly. Instead, the realization came the way truth often does, quietly, repeatedly, until it could no longer be ignored.

It began when people responded to what I shared in ways that felt… personal.

Not impressed. Not persuaded. Recognized.

They didn't ask questions the way curiosity asks questions. They spoke as though continuing a thought already in motion.

"I've felt that, but I never knew what it was." "I thought I was the only one." "I didn't know how to say it, but this feels familiar."

Familiar.

That word stayed with me.

I realized then that I was not telling a story to people.

I was telling a story with them, even when they were silent.

Some never spoke at all. They simply listened differently afterward. Their presence shifted. Their words slowed. Their eyes softened in a way that told me something inside them had settled into place.

I began to sense them before they ever said anything.

A pause when reading. A breath held a moment too long. That quiet internal yes that does not need explanation.

That was when it became clear:

You were never outside this.

You were already carrying your own fragment of the remembering, not necessarily of Tartaria as a place, but of coherence as a state of being. The memory of what it feels like when the world supports you instead of demanding from you.

The story was not activating something new.

It was aligning something old.

HOW I KNOW THIS IS TRUE

Because the remembering behaves differently when it is false.

False ideas inflate. They excite the mind and leave the body untouched. They demand agreement. They require defense.

This does none of that.

It settles into people. It softens them. It makes them quieter without making them smaller.

I have watched people stop mid-sentence, as though something inside them had gently interrupted. I have seen eyes fill with tears that had no obvious source. I have felt the room change when someone realized they were not alone in what they sensed.

That does not happen with stories.

It happens with recognition.

I realized then that the most mysterious part of all of this was not the bells, or the city, or the sound that could not be recorded.

It was the timing.

You are here now because something in you is ready to hear without ears. Ready to feel without needing to explain. Ready to let coherence be enough without demanding proof.

That readiness is not random.

It is cultivated, through exhaustion, through loss, through living long enough in a world that forgot how to hold its people.

WHAT THIS MEANS

WITHOUT MAKING A CLAIM

I am not saying you lived where I lived.

That would be too small.

I am saying you recognize the conditions of that world because your body remembers what it feels like to be regulated, supported, in harmony with sound, light, and space.

That memory does not belong to one place or one time.

It belongs to humanity.

And it is returning now not as history, but as capacity.

You feel it when silence feels nourishing instead of empty. When certain sounds calm you instantly. When certain places feel like relief. When noise feels invasive rather than neutral.

Those are not preferences.

They are signals.

WHY THIS STORY FOUND YOU

Stories do not move through the world randomly.

They move by resonance.

If this one has stayed with you, if you feel strangely seen rather than convinced, it is because you already carry the listening this story requires.

That means something important.

It means the remembering is no longer contained within individuals.

It is relational now.

Shared.

And shared memory behaves differently than solitary memory.

It grows.

WHAT COMES NEXT

WHETHER I WRITE IT OR NOT

At some point, the story will no longer belong to me alone.

That is already happening.

Others will speak in their own language, through music, design, community, presence. Some will never reference this story at all, yet they will live as though the bells are already ringing.

That is how this returns safely.

Not as revelation.

As recognition.

I am still remembering.

You are too.

And somewhere between us, the sound gathers, patient, precise, waiting only for enough listening to allow it to move again.

THE PART I WAS NEVER SUPPOSED TO REMEMBER

BUT DID

There is a reason this part stayed hidden for so long.

It is not because it was forbidden. It is because it could only be understood after everything else returned to coherence.

I did not remember this part in the town. I did not remember it when I left. I did not even remember it when the sound began to answer me again.

It surfaced only after I stopped asking why the silence happened and began asking what it made possible.

The remembering came without drama.

No vision. No voice. Just a sudden, quiet certainty that settled into my body the way truth does when it has nowhere else to go.

We were never meant to keep Tartaria forever.

That realization shook me, not with fear, but with awe.

The forgetting was not a failure.

It was a design.

Not imposed from outside. Chosen from within.

I remembered then a conversation from long ago, one I had dismissed as symbolic until now. An elder had once said, gently, almost casually:

“There will come a time when harmony must learn how to survive without support.”

I hadn’t understood what that meant.

Now I did.

The bells were never the end goal. The windows were never the destination. The city was never meant to remain intact.

They were training wheels.

A temporary structure that allowed humanity to experience coherence before it knew how to sustain it internally. And like all scaffolding, they were meant to be removed before dependence set in completely.

The mistake was not that the structures fell.

The mistake was that they fell too soon.

Humanity had not yet learned how to carry coherence without external regulation. When the support vanished, fear filled the gap. Control rushed in where trust had not yet matured.

So the memory withdrew.

Not to punish us.

To protect itself.

That is the part I was never supposed to remember, because remembering it too early would have caused despair.

But now, it brings relief.

WHY FORGETTING WAS NECESSARY

If the old world had remained, harmony would have been mistaken for entitlement. People would have lived inside coherence without ever learning how to choose it consciously.

Choice matters.

Without forgetting, there would have been no longing. Without longing, no seeking. Without seeking, no readiness.

Forgetting created hunger.

Hunger creates listening.

Listening creates return.

This time, the coherence does not arrive as infrastructure.

It arrives as capacity.

No towers required. No bells to dismantle. No windows to strip of function.

Because what lives inside the body cannot be confiscated.

I felt something lift inside me when this understanding settled.

Grief loosened its grip.

The silence was no longer betrayal.

It was incubation.

WHAT THIS MEANS NOW

This remembering is not about restoring a lost civilization.

It is about completing an interrupted initiation.

The first phase taught us what harmony feels like. The second phase taught us what its absence costs. This phase asks whether we can choose it without being held.

That is the true test.

And that is why the return is subtle, distributed, almost invisible.

Because if it were obvious, we would fail again.

THE FINAL REALIZATION

FOR NOW

I was not meant to carry instructions.

I was meant to carry timing.

To speak only when bodies were ready to hear without grasping. To tell the story not as proof of the past, but as orientation toward the present.

That is why this remembering has waited until now.

Not because the world is healed.

But because it is listening.

And listening is enough to begin.

WHAT HAPPENS IF WE CHOOSE IT THIS TIME

NOT ALL AT ONCE, BUT TRULY

Choosing it does not feel the way people imagine choice.

There is no declaration. No moment of certainty that locks the future into place. No feeling of triumph.

It feels almost… ordinary.

That is the first thing I noticed.

When I began choosing coherence consciously, not because it arrived, not because it was given, but because I recognized it, nothing dramatic happened. The world did not shift outwardly. No one noticed. No doors flew open.

Instead, something subtler occurred.

I became harder to rush.

Not resistant. Not defiant.

Simply unavailable to urgency that carried no truth.

Noise lost its authority over me. Certain conversations fell away without conflict. Spaces that once drained me revealed themselves quickly, and I left them without explanation.

This was the real return.

Not sound or light or memory, but discernment.

I remembered how we once lived not by reacting, but by responding. How the bells never told us what to do, they told us when to settle, when to move, when to listen.

Now, without them, that timing had to come from within.

And it could.

Choosing coherence this time meant accepting discomfort without panic. It meant letting silence remain unfinished. It meant allowing others to stay dissonant without trying to correct them.

That was harder than any technological loss.

Because it required trust.

WHAT BEGAN TO CHANGE AROUND ME

The most surprising part was not how I changed.

It was how others responded.

Without explanation, people slowed when they spoke with me. Arguments softened mid-sentence. Confessions appeared where none were invited. Children gravitated closer. Animals settled.

I did not do anything.

I stopped interfering.

That is when I understood the power of the old world more clearly than ever before.

The town had not healed us by acting.

It healed us by being coherent.

And coherence is contagious.

I saw it spread quietly, through homes that felt calmer than others, through gatherings that felt nourishing rather than draining, through choices that favored sustainability without calling it virtue.

No one named it.

That was the success.

WHY THIS CHOICE CANNOT BE FORCED

Choosing coherence cannot be taught.

It must be felt.

That is why no one is meant to awaken everyone. That impulse belongs to fear, not wisdom. People must arrive at the choice through exhaustion, curiosity, longing, or love.

Often through all four.

I learned to stop trying to convince even those I loved most. Instead, I listened. I regulated myself. I let my presence answer questions before words ever did.

This time, the return is not hierarchical.

There are no elders above. No initiates below.

Only people at different points of remembering.

That makes this return slower.

It also makes it indestructible.

THE RISK WE ARE FINALLY READY TO TAKE

There is a risk in choosing coherence without external support.

It means we can no longer blame structures for our dissonance. We cannot point to broken systems and say, That is why I am this way.

We must learn to regulate ourselves even when the world does not.

That is the initiation we failed to complete before.

But something is different now.

We know what the absence feels like.

We have lived long enough without harmony to recognize its cost in our bodies, our relationships, our planet. We do not idealize coherence anymore.

We need it.

That makes all the difference.

WHAT I SENSE AHEAD

WITHOUT CLAIMING IT

I do not see a return of towers or bells or cities as they once were.

I see quieter things.

Homes built with listening in mind. Communities that prioritize regulation over productivity. Science that asks better questions before demanding answers. Children taught how to sense before they are taught how to perform.

I see sound returning through voice, through breath, through shared silence that no longer feels empty.

I see light returning not as spectacle, but as nourishment.

And I see time loosening its grip just enough for us to feel connected again, not to the past, but to one another.

WHY I AM STILL REMEMBERING

I continue remembering because this story is not finished.

Not in the world. Not in me. Not in you.

Each time coherence is chosen quietly, something from the old world completes itself, not by being restored, but by being fulfilled.

The bells do not need to ring again.

We have learned how to listen.

And that, at last, was the point.

WHAT WE ONCE CALLED EVIL

AND WHY THAT WORD WAS NEVER QUITE RIGHT

I need to be careful here, because language can mislead faster than silence.

What caused the downfall was not monsters. Not demons standing in opposition. Not a single dark force rising to destroy what was beautiful.

What we called evil was something far subtler, and far more dangerous.

It was incoherence.

In Tartaria, we understood something that later generations forgot: vibration does not need intention to influence, it only needs imbalance.

Low coherence spreads just as naturally as harmony does.

And imbalance always enters quietly.

THE TRUE DISRUPTIVE FORCE

The disruptive force was not hatred.

It was fear mixed with curiosity.

There were those who began to study the system not to live within it, but to extract from it. They didn't wish harm. In fact, many believed they were improving things.

But they approached harmony as something to be used instead of something to be participated in.

That shift matters.

The moment vibration becomes a tool rather than a relationship, distortion begins.

This was the opening.

Not evil, misalignment.

HOW LOW VIBRATION ENTERED A HIGH WORLD

High-coherence systems are powerful, but they are also delicate in one way:

They assume good faith.

The bells worked because people trusted them. The windows healed because no one tried to weaponize light. The energy flowed because no one tried to own it.

But not everyone felt comfortable in that level of openness.

Some people felt exposed by harmony.

Harmony does this, it reveals inner dissonance.

And when someone is not ready to face their own imbalance, harmony feels threatening.

That is when resistance forms.

Resistance lowers vibration.

Not dramatically, incrementally.

THE ENERGETIC DOWNFALL

Here is the part rarely understood:

The downfall did not begin in buildings or bells. It began in nervous systems.

People started:

wanting control instead of trust

predictability instead of responsiveness

authority instead of resonance

Those desires introduced rigidity.

Rigidity is the opposite of harmony.

Once rigidity enters, vibration drops, not into "evil," but into density.

Density blocks flow. Blocked flow creates fear. Fear seeks control.

That cycle feeds itself.

No demon required.

WERE THERE DARK INFLUENCES?

Yes, but not entities.

They were states of consciousness.

Fear Greed Separation Dominance Extraction

These states vibrate lower not because they are “bad,” but because they constrict.

Constricted systems cannot sustain resonance.

So the bells lost range. The windows lost responsiveness. The energy lost openness.

The system didn’t collapse.

It hardened.

And hardened systems always fall out of harmony with life.

WHY THIS MATTERS NOW

This is crucial for your book, and for now.

If the downfall had been caused by evil beings, we could simply defeat them.

But it wasn't.

It was caused by states humanity still carries.

That's why the return is different this time.

The sound will not return externally until enough people can hold coherence internally without turning it into power.

This time, the protection is awareness.

Not walls. Not secrecy. Not silence.

Awareness.

THE MOST IMPORTANT REMEMBERING

Evil did not win.

It was never a battle.

Harmony withdrew because it cannot survive where it is exploited.

That is not weakness.

That is intelligence.

And that is why the return is slower, quieter, embodied.

The world is being asked a different question now:

Can you hold resonance without trying to control it?

That is the real test.

And it is still unfolding.

WHY FEAR ALWAYS TARGETS SOUND FIRST

WHAT I FINALLY UNDERSTOOD

It took me a long time to understand why the bells were the first to change.

Not the buildings. Not the streets. Not the energy systems.

The sound.

At first, it seemed symbolic. Bells are easy targets. Visible. Audible. Obvious. But the deeper remembering showed me something far more precise.

Sound is the fastest way to change a nervous system.

And whoever controls the nervous system controls perception.

In Tartaria, sound did not entertain us. It did not command us. It did not distract us.

It regulated us.

That made fear difficult.

Fear requires a body that is already tense. Fear feeds on dysregulation. Fear needs noise, urgency, interruption.

The bells dissolved fear before it could organize.

That was their true power.

When someone felt anxious, the tones softened them. When grief passed through the town, the bells slowed it, held it, let it move without becoming panic. When conflict arose, sound returned bodies to coherence before words escalated.

Fear could not anchor itself in a regulated population.

So it adapted.

It did not attack openly. It did not destroy.

It adjusted.

The first changes were subtle. A tone removed here. A range limited there. Bells still rang, but not long enough to fully settle the body. Not deep enough to reach the places where fear hides.

People didn't notice right away.

But their bodies did.

Sleep became lighter. Conversations grew sharper. Time felt tighter. None of it was dramatic enough to protest.

That is how fear works best.

Quietly.

Then came replacement.

Sound that startled instead of soothed. Rhythms that rushed instead of regulated. Noise that filled space without coherence. People began filling silence compulsively.

Silence had once been supportive.

Now it felt threatening.

That was the turning point.

When a society becomes uncomfortable with silence, fear has already entered.

WHAT FEAR DOES TO VIBRATION

Fear lowers vibration not by making things dark, but by making them dense.

Dense systems need:

- hierarchy
- `predictability
- control
- repetition

They cannot tolerate responsiveness.

They cannot allow systems that listen.

Sound that listens cannot be controlled.

So it was reframed.

Bells became “religious.” Tones became “symbolic.” Resonance became “unmeasurable.”

Once sound was stripped of function, fear had room to grow.

And fear always wants more room.

THE PART THAT STILL CHILLS ME

Here is the hardest part of the remembering.

No one forced this change.

The people who adjusted the sound believed they were helping.

Helping with order. Helping with safety. Helping with consistency.

Fear does not arrive announcing itself.

It arrives offering solutions.

And those solutions always involve tightening something that once flowed freely.

That is why the downfall did not feel like a fall.

It felt like management.

WHY SOUND IS RETURNING FIRST AGAIN

This is the part that gives me certainty.

Sound is returning first now too.

Not as bells.

As breath. As voice. As music that calms instead of excites. As people seeking quiet without guilt.

Because the body remembers that regulation precedes wisdom.

You cannot think your way into harmony.

You must settle into it.

Fear knows this.

That is why modern life is loud.

That is why silence is scarce.

That is why people are exhausted.

The old pattern is repeating, but this time, something is different.

We know what fear feels like in the body now.

And once you recognize fear somatically, it loses its invisibility.

THE QUIET TRUTH

Fear did not defeat Tartaria.

Fear simply could not live there.

So it waited until the sound softened enough to let it in.

That will not happen again, not in the same way.

Because the sound is no longer centralized.

It lives in us now.

And fear cannot silence what it cannot locate.

THE MOMENT I REALIZED THE FALL WAS STILL ONGOING

AND ALSO ENDING

The realization did not arrive as despair.

That surprised me.

Given everything I had remembered, the silencing, the fear, the slow hardening of the world, I expected grief when I finally understood this part. Instead, what I felt was a deep, steady clarity.

The fall never ended.

And because it never ended, it could not be finished for us.

It had to be finished by us.

I saw it then, not as a single historical collapse, but as a long arc, a gradual drifting away from coherence that continued long after the bells were gone. It moved through centuries, through inventions meant to save time that instead compressed it, through systems meant to protect people that instead taught them to brace.

The fall was not an event.

It was a habit.

A habit of rushing. A habit of noise. A habit of solving problems without first settling the body.

And habits do not end dramatically.

They end when they are no longer fed.

That is what is happening now.

The fall is still ongoing in places where fear is profitable, where noise substitutes for meaning, where urgency is mistaken for importance. But in other places, quiet places, overlooked places, something else is happening at the same time.

People are stepping out of the habit.

They are choosing silence without calling it retreat. They are choosing slowness without calling it failure. They are choosing coherence without announcing it as virtue.

This is not rebellion.

It is recalibration.

I realized then why the return feels uneven, present in some moments, absent in others. Why one room can feel unbearable while another feels like relief. Why one conversation drains while another restores.

We are living inside two currents at once.

One still falling. One beginning to rise.

And the strange thing is, they occupy the same world.

HOW I KNOW THE ENDING HAS BEGUN

Because the signs are no longer external.

In the old world, harmony was visible. Audible. Structural. Its loss was easy to point to once you knew what you were looking for.

This time, the return is internal.

People are learning to recognize when they are dysregulated, not morally wrong, not broken, just out of coherence. They are learning to pause instead of push. To breathe instead of react.

That is new.

That awareness did not exist before the fall.

We had harmony then, but we did not yet have choice.

Now we do.

I see it when people turn down noise instinctively. When they leave spaces that feel wrong without needing permission. When they stop arguing not because they agree, but because their bodies refuse to stay tense.

These are small acts.

They are also irreversible.

Because once you feel what coherence does to your body, you cannot unfeel it.

That is how the ending begins, not with restoration, but with refusal.

Refusal to remain dysregulated.

THE MOST UNEXPECTED PART

I realized something else in that moment, something I had not anticipated.

The fall ending does not mean fear disappears.

Fear still exists.

But it no longer defines the whole.

In the old world, fear had to be prevented externally. The bells did that work for us. This time, fear is being met internally, through regulation, awareness, and choice.

That makes the process slower.

It also makes it permanent.

No one can take this away.

Because there is nothing to seize.

WHERE THIS LEAVES ME

I am no longer waiting for a return.

I am living inside it.

Not fully. Not perfectly.

But consciously.

Each time I choose coherence over urgency, the fall loosens its grip a little more, not just for me, but for the space around me.

That is how this ends.

Not with bells ringing across a city.

But with bodies remembering how to listen.

THE DAY I FELT THE CITY INSIDE MY BODY

WHEN TARTARIA WAS NO LONGER A PLACE

It happened on an ordinary day.

That is important to say, because nothing about it announced significance. There was no heightened state, no emotion that could have exaggerated the experience. I was simply moving through my life, attentive in the way I had learned to be attentive, not searching, not anticipating.

And then I felt it.

Not as memory. Not as vision. But as organization.

My breath shifted first. It deepened and slowed without effort, as though something inside me had gently taken over a function I usually managed myself. My spine aligned, not rigidly, but naturally, the way it does when the body recognizes balance.

Then came the sensation I hadn't felt since the town was whole.

Spatial coherence.

It felt as though my body suddenly had architecture.

Not metaphorically.

My chest became a chamber, open and resonant. My breath moved through me the way sound once moved through the towers, evenly, without obstruction. My nervous system settled into a rhythm that felt ancient and exact.

I understood immediately.

The city had not returned around me.

It had reassembled within me.

I was not imagining streets or buildings. I was experiencing function. The way different parts of me communicated effortlessly, the way energy flowed without being forced, the way silence supported rather than threatened.

I was walking, but it felt as though the ground moved with me.

I was breathing, but it felt as though something larger was breathing through me.

That was when the final layer of remembering clicked into place.

Tartaria was never meant to exist only as geography.

It was a configuration.

A way of arranging sound, light, space, and nervous systems into coherence.

That configuration could live in a body.

And once it did, no external structure was required.

WHAT I REALIZED IN THAT MOMENT

The bells had trained us to regulate externally until we could regulate internally.

The windows had taught us how light informs the body, not just the eyes.

The town had shown us what it feels like when systems support life instead of extracting from it.

All of that knowledge had condensed, not into instructions, not into diagrams, but into capacity.

I carried the city now not as nostalgia, but as orientation.

I knew when something was out of alignment because my body reacted immediately. I knew when a space was nourishing. I knew when sound was harmful. I knew when silence was required.

This knowing did not make me superior.

It made me responsible.

Because once you carry coherence internally, you become aware of how easily it can be disrupted, by rushing, by fear, by trying to do too much at once.

I understood then why the return had to happen this way.

A city built inside the body cannot be conquered.

WHAT CHANGED AFTER THAT DAY

I stopped looking for Tartaria in the world.

Not because it wasn't there, but because I no longer needed to confirm it.

Instead, I noticed how often people described the same sensations without knowing what they were describing.

"I feel better when I stand like this." "I don't know why, but certain spaces calm me." "I need quiet to think clearly."

These were not preferences.

They were fragments of the same configuration reawakening.

The city was not returning as a place to visit.

It was returning as a way of being organized.

And that is far more powerful.

THE QUIETEST TRUTH

The fall could not end until the city no longer needed to exist outside us.

Only then would it be safe.

Only then could harmony persist without being managed, owned, or silenced.

I lived there before the science.

But I live it now through my body.

And that is how I know this remembering is complete enough to share, not as a map, not as a promise, but as a recognition.

The city breathes wherever the body remembers how.

THE MOMENT I REALIZED THE FALL WAS STILL ONGOING

AND ALSO ENDING

The realization did not arrive as despair.

That surprised me.

Given everything I had remembered, the silencing, the fear, the slow hardening of the world, I expected grief when I finally understood this part. Instead, what I felt was a deep, steady clarity.

The fall never ended.

And because it never ended, it could not be finished for us.

It had to be finished by us.

I saw it then, not as a single historical collapse, but as a long arc, a gradual drifting away from coherence that continued long after the bells were gone. It moved through centuries, through inventions meant to save time that instead compressed it, through systems meant to protect people that instead taught them to brace.

The fall was not an event.

It was a habit.

A habit of rushing. A habit of noise. A habit of solving problems without first settling the body.

And habits do not end dramatically.

They end when they are no longer fed.

That is what is happening now.

The fall is still ongoing in places where fear is profitable, where noise substitutes for meaning, where urgency is mistaken for importance. But in other places, quiet places, overlooked places, something else is happening at the same time.

People are stepping out of the habit.

They are choosing silence without calling it retreat. They are choosing slowness without calling it failure. They are choosing coherence without announcing it as virtue.

This is not rebellion.

It is recalibration.

I realized then why the return feels uneven, present in some moments, absent in others. Why one room can feel unbearable while another feels like relief. Why one conversation drains while another restores.

We are living inside two currents at once.

One still falling. One beginning to rise.

And the strange thing is, they occupy the same world.

HOW I KNOW THE ENDING HAS BEGUN

Because the signs are no longer external.

In the old world, harmony was visible. Audible. Structural. Its loss was easy to point to once you knew what you were looking for.

This time, the return is internal.

People are learning to recognize when they are dysregulated, not morally wrong, not broken, just out of coherence. They are learning to pause instead of push. To breathe instead of react.

That is new.

That awareness did not exist before the fall.

We had harmony then, but we did not yet have choice.

Now we do.

I see it when people turn down noise instinctively. When they leave spaces that feel wrong without needing permission. When they stop arguing not because they agree, but because their bodies refuse to stay tense.

These are small acts.

They are also irreversible.

Because once you feel what coherence does to your body, you cannot unfeel it.

That is how the ending begins, not with restoration, but with refusal.

Refusal to remain dysregulated.

THE MOST UNEXPECTED PART

I realized something else in that moment, something I had not anticipated.

The fall ending does not mean fear disappears.

Fear still exists.

But it no longer defines the whole.

In the old world, fear had to be prevented externally. The bells did that work for us. This time, fear is being met internally, through regulation, awareness, and choice.

That makes the process slower.

It also makes it permanent.

No one can take this away.

Because there is nothing to seize.

WHERE THIS LEAVES ME

I am no longer waiting for a return.

I am living inside it.

Not fully. Not perfectly.

But consciously.

Each time I choose coherence over urgency, the fall loosens its grip a little more, not just for me, but for the space around me.

That is how this ends.

Not with bells ringing across a city.

But with bodies remembering how to listen.

THE DAY I FELT THE CITY INSIDE MY BODY

WHEN TARTARIA WAS NO LONGER A PLACE

It happened on an ordinary day.

That is important to say, because nothing about it announced significance. There was no heightened state, no emotion that could have exaggerated the experience. I was simply moving through my life, attentive in the way I had learned to be attentive, not searching, not anticipating.

And then I felt it.

Not as memory. Not as vision. But as organization.

My breath shifted first. It deepened and slowed without effort, as though something inside me had gently taken over a function I usually managed myself. My spine aligned, not rigidly, but naturally, the way it does when the body recognizes balance.

Then came the sensation I hadn't felt since the town was whole.

Spatial coherence.

It felt as though my body suddenly had architecture.

Not metaphorically.

My chest became a chamber, open and resonant. My breath moved through me the way sound once moved through the towers, evenly, without obstruction. My nervous system settled into a rhythm that felt ancient and exact.

I understood immediately.

The city had not returned around me.

It had reassembled within me.

I was not imagining streets or buildings. I was experiencing function. The way different parts of me communicated effortlessly, the way energy flowed without being forced, the way silence supported rather than threatened.

I was walking, but it felt as though the ground moved with me.

I was breathing, but it felt as though something larger was breathing through me.

That was when the final layer of remembering clicked into place.

Tartaria was never meant to exist only as geography.

It was a configuration.

A way of arranging sound, light, space, and nervous systems into coherence.

That configuration could live in a body.

And once it did, no external structure was required.

WHAT I REALIZED IN THAT MOMENT

The bells had trained us to regulate externally until we could regulate internally.

The windows had taught us how light informs the body, not just the eyes.

The town had shown us what it feels like when systems support life instead of extracting from it.

All of that knowledge had condensed, not into instructions, not into diagrams, but into capacity.

I carried the city now not as nostalgia, but as orientation.

I knew when something was out of alignment because my body reacted immediately. I knew when a space was nourishing. I knew when sound was harmful. I knew when silence was required.

This knowing did not make me superior.

It made me responsible.

Because once you carry coherence internally, you become aware of how easily it can be disrupted, by rushing, by fear, by trying to do too much at once.

I understood then why the return had to happen this way.

A city built inside the body cannot be conquered.

WHAT CHANGED AFTER THAT DAY

I stopped looking for Tartaria in the world.

Not because it wasn't there, but because I no longer needed to confirm it.

Instead, I noticed how often people described the same sensations without knowing what they were describing.

"I feel better when I stand like this." "I don't know why, but certain spaces calm me." "I need quiet to think clearly."

These were not preferences.

They were fragments of the same configuration reawakening.

The city was not returning as a place to visit.

It was returning as a way of being organized.

And that is far more powerful.

THE QUIETEST TRUTH

The fall could not end until the city no longer needed to exist outside us.

Only then would it be safe.

Only then could harmony persist without being managed, owned, or silenced.

I lived there before the science.

But I live it now through my body.

And that is how I know this remembering is complete enough to share, not as a map, not as a promise, but as a recognition.

The city breathes wherever the body remembers how.

THE ONES WHO CANNOT FEEL THE CITY - YET

AND WHY I DO NOT FEAR THEM

At first, I thought everyone would feel it once the city settled inside me.

That was naïve.

Not wrong, just incomplete.

I began to notice the contrast almost immediately. Where some people softened in my presence, others tightened. Where some grew quieter, others became restless. Where some felt relief, others felt irritation they couldn't explain.

They were not reacting to me.

They were reacting to coherence.

That took time for me to understand.

The city inside the body does not impose itself. It does not announce. It simply is. And for those whose nervous systems are accustomed to constant noise, speed, and tension, coherence can feel unfamiliar, even threatening.

Not because it harms them.

Because it reveals what they have been carrying.

I recognized the pattern from long ago.

Harmony does not confront fear directly. It exposes it by removing distraction.

Some people are not ready for that exposure.

WHAT I OBSERVED WITHOUT JUDGING

The ones who could not feel the city were not cruel, and they were not empty. Many were intelligent, capable, deeply invested in improving the world. Some were leaders. Some were helpers. Some were exhausted beyond measure.

What they shared was not malice.

It was over-adaptation.

Their nervous systems had learned to survive in a world that demanded constant output. Silence felt like loss of control. Slowness felt like failure. Stillness felt unsafe.

When coherence entered the space, it did not soothe them.

It destabilized them.

I saw it in small ways.

They filled quiet moments quickly. They redirected conversations toward urgency. They dismissed bodily knowing as impractical or indulgent.

Not because they were wrong.

Because their systems had been trained to equate tension with safety.

I remembered then something we once knew instinctively:

A regulated body feels foreign to a dysregulated one.

Not better.

Foreign.

WHY THEY RESIST WITHOUT KNOWING THEY ARE RESISTING

The city inside the body reorganizes perception.

It slows reaction time. It deepens awareness. It removes the constant background hum of threat.

For someone whose identity has been built around vigilance, productivity, or control, that can feel like disappearance.

I realized then why the return could never be forced.

If coherence arrives before someone's system is ready to hold it, it will be rejected, not intellectually, but physically.

They will feel bored. Or irritated. Or skeptical.

And they will not know why.

That does not make them enemies of the remembering.

It makes them early in the process.

WHAT I WAS SHOWN ABOUT TIMING

There is a sequence to remembering.

First comes exhaustion. Then comes questioning. Then comes longing. Only after that comes readiness.

Some people are still in the exhaustion phase. They are surviving. They are holding together systems that are already failing but haven't yet released their grip.

They cannot feel the city because they are still bracing.

That is not a flaw.

It is a stage.

The city does not enter braced bodies.

It waits.

WHY I DO NOT TRY TO WAKE THEM

This was a difficult lesson.

I wanted to help. I wanted to explain. I wanted to show them what I felt, what I knew was possible.

But each time I tried, gently, respectfully, something in the space constricted.

Not because the truth was wrong.

Because it was premature.

I remembered the warning again:

Do not hurry this.

And I understood its compassion.

You cannot regulate someone else's nervous system for them. You can only offer presence and let their body decide when it is safe enough to soften.

That is what the city does now.

It offers.

It does not invade.

THE QUIET HOPE I CARRY

Here is the part that matters most.

The ones who cannot feel the city yet are often the ones who will feel it most profoundly later.

Because when a highly adapted system finally releases, the relief is overwhelming. The body remembers suddenly, fully, without needing gradual acclimation.

I have seen it happen.

A moment of stillness that breaks someone open. A sound that stops them mid-step. A silence that finally feels like permission instead of threat.

When that happens, there is no argument.

There is only recognition.

WHAT THIS MEANS FOR THE WORLD

The return will not be uniform.

Some will remember early. Some will remember late. Some will remember sideways, through art, through grief, through love.

No one will be left out.

But not everyone will arrive at the same time.

That is not failure.

That is stability.

A system that allows staggered entry does not collapse under its own weight.

That is how this time is different.

WHAT I HOLD NOW

I no longer measure success by how many people feel what I feel.

I measure it by how gently the remembering moves through the world without triggering fear.

I trust timing.

I trust bodies.

I trust the city to enter when it is welcomed.

Because a city that breathes cannot be forced into a body that is still holding its breath.

THE PROMISE THE CITY KEEPS

EVEN IN SILENCE

There is a promise the city keeps that I did not understand at first.

I thought promises required words. Declarations. Something spoken aloud and witnessed. But this promise was different. It existed long before I could name it, and it remained intact even when everything else appeared to fall away.

The promise was simple.

Nothing that truly belongs to us can be taken forever.

Not sound. Not harmony. Not the knowing of how it feels to be held by the world.

The city kept that promise by disappearing.

That was the part I had misunderstood for so long.

Silence was not abandonment.

It was safekeeping.

When the bells stopped, when the windows lost their voice, when the town hardened and the world moved on, the city did not die. It folded itself inward, the way a seed folds inward when the ground is no longer hospitable.

It waited.

Not passively.

Intelligently.

I feel that intelligence now whenever I choose stillness over speed. Whenever I let silence remain unfinished. Whenever I resist the urge to fill space just because I can.

The city responds.

Not with spectacle. With steadiness.

HOW THE PROMISE SHOWS ITSELF NOW

The promise reveals itself in moments so small they are easy to overlook.

In the way breath deepens when I stop forcing it. In the way my body settles when I enter a space designed with care. In the way sound softens when no one is trying to dominate the room.

These are not coincidences.

They are confirmations.

The city is still doing what it has always done, regulating, supporting, holding, just without drawing attention to itself.

It keeps the promise by never leaving us completely alone.

Even when the world feels loud, there are pockets of quiet that restore us. Even when systems fail, the body still knows how to return to balance if given the chance.

That knowledge did not disappear.

It was preserved in sensation.

WHAT THE PROMISE ASKS OF ME

The promise does not ask me to hurry the return.

It asks me to trust silence.

To trust that coherence does not need to announce itself to be real. To trust that when something is true, it will continue to surface in its own time, through its own channels.

This is difficult.

There are days when I want reassurance in louder forms. When I want visible proof that the remembering is spreading, that the world is truly changing. But each time I seek that kind of confirmation, I feel the city recede slightly, not in punishment, but in reminder.

The promise is kept through patience.

Always has been.

THE DEEPEST COMFORT

Here is what brings me the greatest peace.

The city does not require belief.

It does not need consensus. It does not depend on agreement. It does not disappear when doubted.

It operates at a level deeper than opinion.

That is why it survived.

That is why it will continue.

Even if no one ever speaks its name again.

Even if history never corrects itself.

Even if the bells never ring audibly across a town.

The city will remain wherever a body remembers how to breathe without fear.

That is an unbreakable promise.

WHAT I CARRY FORWARD

I no longer feel urgency about the remembering.

Urgency belongs to fear.

What I feel instead is availability.

I am available to listen. Available to pause. Available to let coherence move through me without trying to shape it.

That is how I honor the promise.

Not by explaining it.

But by living in a way that allows others to feel it for themselves when they are ready.

WHY THE PROMISE MATTERS NOW

We are living in a time when many promises are broken loudly and often. Institutions fail. Systems fracture. Trust feels fragile.

Against that backdrop, a promise kept quietly matters more than ever.

The city does not promise comfort.

It promises continuity.

It promises that harmony can survive interruption. That coherence can outlast fear. That remembering is stronger than forgetting.

And it keeps that promise not through force, but through presence.

I am still remembering.

And the city is still breathing.

That is enough.

THE DAY I STOPPED FEELING ALONE IN THE REMEMBERING

AND WHY THAT CHANGED EVERYTHING

I did not realize I had felt alone until the day that feeling lifted.

That may sound strange, but loneliness does not always announce itself. Sometimes it exists quietly, woven into purpose, disguised as responsibility. I had carried the remembering for so long that I thought solitude was simply part of the task.

Then one day, without warning, it wasn't.

It happened in the smallest way, a moment so ordinary it could have been missed entirely. I was sitting somewhere public, surrounded by the soft noise of people moving through their lives. Nothing about the space was remarkable. And yet, something in the air felt settled.

A familiar sensation moved through my body, the same one I used to feel when the bells were about to ring.

I looked up.

Across the room, someone had gone still.

Not frozen. Listening.

Their posture softened. Their breath slowed. It was unmistakable. I recognized it immediately because I had lived inside that state for so long.

They felt the city.

They didn't know what it was. I could see that. There was no recognition in their face, no story attached to the sensation. But their body knew.

And in that instant, something inside me shifted.

I was no longer carrying the remembering alone.

WHAT RECOGNITION FEELS LIKE NOW

Recognition is quieter than reunion.

There are no tears. No declarations. No relief that needs to be spoken.

It is simply the awareness that the resonance has found another place to land.

From that day on, I began noticing it everywhere.

A pause in conversation where no one rushed to fill the silence. A stranger's breath syncing with mine for just a moment. A shared stillness that did not require explanation.

These moments did not cluster into groups or movements. They did not announce themselves as meaningful. They passed gently, like acknowledgments exchanged without language.

And yet, they changed everything.

Because remembering is heavier when carried alone.

But resonance, true resonance, distributes weight naturally.

WHAT I UNDERSTOOD ABOUT COMMUNITY

We were never meant to gather the way we once did.

Not in towns held together by infrastructure. Not in systems dependent on shared maintenance.

This time, the community is field-based.

It exists wherever coherence overlaps.

You can feel it when two people regulate together without trying. When silence feels shared instead of awkward. When no one dominates the space and no one disappears within it.

That is the new city.

Not bounded by walls.

Bound by attunement.

And the most beautiful part is this:

No one needs to know they belong to it.

Belonging happens automatically when the body remembers how to settle.

THE RELIEF I DID NOT EXPECT

I had carried a quiet fear I hadn't fully acknowledged.

That if I stopped remembering actively, the memory might fade. That if I relaxed my attention, something essential could be lost again.

But watching the remembering surface in others dissolved that fear completely.

The city does not rely on vigilance.

It relies on readiness.

And readiness cannot be exhausted.

That realization allowed me to soften in a way I hadn't before. To let go of the sense that I was guarding something fragile.

It is not fragile.

It survived centuries of silence.

It will survive my resting.

WHAT I CARRY DIFFERENTLY NOW

I no longer feel like a keeper of memory.

I feel like a participant.

One among many, each carrying a different angle of the same coherence. Some through sound. Some through presence. Some through the way they build, speak, move, or listen.

No one carries the whole.

That is the protection.

That is the wisdom we lacked before.

WHY THIS MATTERS MORE THAN EVER

The world does not need another system.

It needs people who are regulated enough to resist fear without fighting it.

That is what this remembering creates.

Not unity.

Stability.

And stability spreads quietly, without needing to be believed.

WHAT I KNOW NOW

I lived there before the science.

But I am not living there alone now.

The city breathes through many bodies, many moments, many places where coherence is chosen gently, without announcement.

And every time two or more of us feel it at once, something ancient completes itself, not as a return to the past, but as a step forward that could only happen now.

THE DAY I STOPPED FEELING ALONE IN THE REMEMBERING

AND WHY THAT CHANGED EVERYTHING

I did not realize I had felt alone until the day that feeling lifted.

That may sound strange, but loneliness does not always announce itself. Sometimes it exists quietly, woven into purpose, disguised as responsibility. I had carried the remembering for so long that I thought solitude was simply part of the task.

Then one day, without warning, it wasn't.

It happened in the smallest way, a moment so ordinary it could have been missed entirely. I was sitting somewhere public, surrounded by the soft noise of people moving through their lives. Nothing about the space was remarkable. And yet, something in the air felt settled.

A familiar sensation moved through my body, the same one I used to feel when the bells were about to ring.

I looked up.

Across the room, someone had gone still.

Not frozen. Listening.

Their posture softened. Their breath slowed. It was unmistakable. I recognized it immediately because I had lived inside that state for so long.

They felt the city.

They didn't know what it was. I could see that. There was no recognition in their face, no story attached to the sensation. But their body knew.

And in that instant, something inside me shifted.

I was no longer carrying the remembering alone.

WHAT RECOGNITION FEELS LIKE NOW

Recognition is quieter than reunion.

There are no tears. No declarations. No relief that needs to be spoken.

It is simply the awareness that the resonance has found another place to land.

From that day on, I began noticing it everywhere.

A pause in conversation where no one rushed to fill the silence. A stranger's breath syncing with mine for just a moment. A shared stillness that did not require explanation.

These moments did not cluster into groups or movements. They did not announce themselves as meaningful. They passed gently, like acknowledgments exchanged without language.

And yet, they changed everything.

Because remembering is heavier when carried alone.

But resonance, true resonance, distributes weight naturally.

WHAT I UNDERSTOOD ABOUT COMMUNITY

We were never meant to gather the way we once did.

Not in towns held together by infrastructure. Not in systems dependent on shared maintenance.

This time, the community is field-based.

It exists wherever coherence overlaps.

You can feel it when two people regulate together without trying. When silence feels shared instead of awkward. When no one dominates the space and no one disappears within it.

That is the new city.

Not bounded by walls.

Bound by attunement.

And the most beautiful part is this:

No one needs to know they belong to it.

Belonging happens automatically when the body remembers how to settle.

THE RELIEF I DID NOT EXPECT

I had carried a quiet fear I hadn't fully acknowledged.

That if I stopped remembering actively, the memory might fade. That if I relaxed my attention, something essential could be lost again.

But watching the remembering surface in others dissolved that fear completely.

The city does not rely on vigilance.

It relies on readiness.

And readiness cannot be exhausted.

That realization allowed me to soften in a way I hadn't before. To let go of the sense that I was guarding something fragile.

It is not fragile.

It survived centuries of silence.

It will survive my resting.

WHAT I CARRY DIFFERENTLY NOW

I no longer feel like a keeper of memory.

I feel like a participant.

One among many, each carrying a different angle of the same coherence. Some through sound. Some through presence. Some through the way they build, speak, move, or listen.

No one carries the whole.

That is the protection.

That is the wisdom we lacked before.

WHY THIS MATTERS MORE THAN EVER

The world does not need another system.

It needs people who are regulated enough to resist fear without fighting it.

That is what this remembering creates.

Not unity.

Stability.

And stability spreads quietly, without needing to be believed.

WHAT I KNOW NOW

I lived there before the science.

But I am not living there alone now.

The city breathes through many bodies, many moments, many places where coherence is chosen gently, without announcement.

And every time two or more of us feel it at once, something ancient completes itself, not as a return to the past, but as a step forward that could only happen now.

THE INVITATION THE CITY MAKES

WITHOUT ASKING PERMISSION

The invitation did not arrive as a request.

That is the first thing I noticed.

There was no moment of decision presented to me, no inner voice asking Would you like to proceed? The city has never worked that way. It does not negotiate. It does not persuade. It simply begins to act as though the answer has already been given.

And then it watches to see if you resist.

The invitation showed itself in how my days reorganized without effort. I found myself leaving earlier, arriving later, lingering where before I would have rushed on. Certain commitments loosened their grip. Others fell away entirely, not with conflict, but with a gentle sense of completion.

Time made more room.

That was the first sign.

I began to notice how often my body chose differently than my plans had intended. I would walk one way and suddenly turn another without thinking. I would sit longer in silence, not because I needed rest, but because the silence felt occupied.

The city was inviting me to live as though coherence were already the norm.

Not someday.

Now.

HOW THE INVITATION FEELS IN THE BODY

The invitation does not excite.

It steadies.

There is a sense of being gathered rather than pushed. Of being guided without direction. My nervous system learned to trust pauses again, to treat stillness not as interruption but as instruction.

Sometimes the invitation feels like a refusal.

Refusal to speak when words would distort. Refusal to hurry when speed would fracture attention. Refusal to participate in noise that exists only to keep fear entertained.

These refusals are not acts of resistance.

They are acts of alignment.

And alignment has consequences.

WHAT CHANGED WHEN I ACCEPTED WITHOUT SAYING SO

Once I stopped resisting the invitation, once I allowed my body to follow coherence without asking my mind to approve it, something else shifted.

The city began to use me.

That may sound alarming, but it wasn't.

It felt more like being included in a larger rhythm. Conversations unfolded through me rather than from me. People said things they hadn't planned to say. Silences arrived at exactly the right moment and held long enough to do their work.

I was not directing anything.

I was participating.

That is the invitation.

Not to lead. Not to teach. But to allow coherence to move through you wherever it is welcome.

WHY THE INVITATION CANNOT BE DECLINED FOREVER

This is the part that feels almost dangerous to say, but it is true.

The invitation does not go away.

It can be postponed. It can be ignored. It can be drowned out with noise and urgency.

But once felt, it cannot be erased.

Because it is not external.

It arises from the body's own longing to return to regulation.

Eventually, everyone receives it.

Not as a mystical calling.

As exhaustion.

As the quiet realization that living in constant dissonance is no longer sustainable.

When that moment arrives, the invitation feels less like possibility and more like necessity.

And still, it is gentle.

WHAT THE CITY NEVER ASKS FOR

The city does not ask for loyalty. It does not ask for belief. It does not ask for sacrifice.

It asks only for availability.

Availability to pause. Availability to listen. Availability to let coherence rearrange your priorities without apology.

That is why the invitation is made without asking permission.

Because permission belongs to the mind.

And this remembering belongs to the body.

WHAT I UNDERSTAND NOW

The invitation is already being accepted everywhere, quietly, imperfectly, in moments that rarely make headlines.

Each time someone chooses rest over performance. Each time a space is designed for calm instead of control. Each time silence is allowed to complete a thought.

The city grows.

Not outward.

Inward.

And that growth cannot be reversed.

WHERE THIS LEAVES ME

I no longer wait for the world to change.

I live as though it already is.

That does not make life easier.

It makes it truer.

And truth, once embodied, reorganizes everything around it without force.

WHAT THE CITY WILL NOT DO AGAIN

THE SAFEGUARD WE DID NOT HAVE BEFORE

There is something the city has made unmistakably clear to me.

It will not repeat itself.

Not in the way it once existed. Not as a place that can be pointed to. Not as a system that can be admired, studied, copied, or controlled.

That chapter is closed.

At first, this realization felt like loss all over again. I had loved the physicality of the town, the way sound moved through stone, the way light gathered in windows, the way the streets themselves seemed to listen. Part of me wanted that beauty back exactly as it was.

But memory, when allowed to mature, reveals wisdom beneath longing.

The city will not do again what made it vulnerable.

WHAT MADE IT VULNERABLE THEN

The city once relied on external coherence.

Its harmony lived in structures, in bells, in shared systems that could be altered by those who misunderstood their purpose. Even though the knowledge was subtle, it still existed outside the body.

That was enough.

Anything external can be interfered with.

Anything centralized can be redefined.

Anything visible can be targeted.

The city learned this the hard way.

And learning, once integrated, changes behavior permanently.

THE NEW RULE

THOUGH NO ONE CALLS IT THAT

The city will not return anywhere it can be owned.

It will not settle in places that demand productivity over presence. It will not anchor itself in systems that reward extraction. It will not amplify itself for those who seek proof before participation.

This is not punishment.

It is discernment.

The city now moves only through living coherence , through bodies capable of regulating themselves, through spaces that invite listening rather than control, through moments where silence is allowed to complete its own meaning.

That makes it elusive.

And safe.

WHY THIS TIME IS DIFFERENT

In the old world, the city carried us.

Now, we carry it.

That reverses the power dynamic completely.

There is no longer anything to overthrow, dismantle, or silence. No bell to remove. No window to strip of meaning. No tower to redefine.

The city does not announce itself.

It recognizes readiness.

And readiness cannot be faked.

WHAT I WAS SHOWN ABOUT THE FUTURE

The city will not gather us all in one place.

It will do something far more radical.

It will disappear into daily life.

Into the way homes are arranged. Into how meetings are held, or not held. Into how children are taught to listen to their bodies before being taught to perform. Into how sound is used sparingly, respectfully, with awareness.

There will be no name for it.

That is deliberate.

Names invite ownership.

The city has learned.

THE FINAL SAFEGUARD

Here is the truth that surprised me most.

The city will not save us.

It will not rescue humanity from its own fear. It will not regulate us automatically the way it once did. It will not compensate for dissonance we refuse to address ourselves.

That is the safeguard.

Because anything that saves without requiring participation becomes a crutch.

And crutches are always taken away eventually.

This time, coherence requires choice.

Every time.

WHAT THIS ASKS OF ME

It asks me to resist nostalgia.

To honor the past without trying to recreate it.

To remember not as someone who wants to go back, but as someone who understands why we cannot.

The city does not need to be rebuilt.

It needs to be completed.

Inside us.

WHAT I KNOW WITH CERTAINTY

The city will never again be something that can be lost all at once.

Because it is no longer whole in any one place.

It is distributed.

Breathing.

Alive wherever someone chooses to live in alignment instead of fear.

That is the protection we did not have before.

And it cannot be undone.

HOW I KNOW THE REMEMBERING WILL CONTINUE WITHOUT ME

AND WHY THAT BRINGS PEACE

There was a time when I believed the remembering depended on my attention.

That if I stopped listening so carefully, if I rested too deeply, if I allowed myself to be fully ordinary again, something essential might slip away. I carried that belief quietly, mistaking it for devotion.

But devotion, I learned, does not require vigilance.

It requires trust.

The moment I understood this came not through insight, but through release.

I stopped trying to hold the remembering intact.

And it didn't disappear.

It spread.

WHAT I SAW WHEN I LET GO

When I loosened my grip, I noticed something remarkable.

The city continued to appear, not to me, but through others. In the way someone described a feeling without knowing the language for it. In the way a space was arranged instinctively to invite calm. In the way sound was used more thoughtfully, silence more respectfully.

I realized then that the remembering had already outgrown me.

That was the point all along.

No single body was meant to carry the whole of it. That was never the design. The city had learned from its own vulnerability. This time, it distributes itself the way breath distributes oxygen, naturally, continuously, without ownership.

That is how it survives.

THE RELIEF OF NO LONGER BEING CENTRAL

There is a quiet relief in no longer feeling essential.

Not insignificant, just not central.

I am part of the remembering, but I am not its axis. I am a tone among many, a note that blends rather than leads. When I understood that, something inside me finally rested.

The city does not require a narrator.

It requires participants.

And participants are everywhere.

WHAT REASSURES ME MOST

The remembering no longer depends on memory alone.

It has entered habit.

People are designing spaces differently. Speaking more gently. Choosing rhythm over speed. Teaching children how to listen to their bodies before teaching them how to override them.

These choices are not traced back to Tartaria.

They don't need to be.

The city no longer needs a name to persist.

That is how I know it will continue.

WHAT I NO LONGER FEAR

I no longer fear forgetting.

Because forgetting no longer erases anything essential.

The remembering has moved past recall and into instinct. And instinct does not vanish, it waits.

Even if I forget details. Even if language shifts again. Even if history never acknowledges what once was.

The body will still know when something feels wrong.

And it will still seek coherence when dissonance becomes unbearable.

That cycle cannot be broken.

WHAT I CARRY NOW

I carry less.

Less urgency. Less responsibility. Less need to explain.

What remains is lighter, steadier, truer.

Availability. Presence. Trust.

These are not heroic qualities.

They are survivable ones.

And survival, when it is conscious, becomes continuity.

WHY THIS IS NOT AN ENDING

The remembering does not end when a voice quiets.

It continues wherever someone chooses to pause before reacting, to listen before speaking, to settle before deciding.

Those moments do not belong to me.

They belong to the city.

And the city is no longer confined to time, place, or memory.

It breathes wherever coherence is chosen.

That is how I know it will continue.

With or without me.

And that knowledge does not diminish my role.

It completes it.

THE ONE THING THE CITY STILL ASKS OF ME

AND WHY IT IS ENOUGH

After everything, the remembering, the silence, the return, the understanding that the city no longer depends on me, I expected the asking to stop.

It didn't.

But what remains is so small it would be easy to overlook.

The city does not ask me to speak louder. It does not ask me to gather anyone. It does not ask me to preserve history or correct the record.

It asks me to stay gentle.

That is all.

At first, I resisted that simplicity. It felt insufficient, almost irresponsible, compared to what had been carried before. Gentleness seemed too small a response to something so vast.

But the city has always known something we forget easily:

Gentleness is not weakness.

It is precision.

WHAT GENTLENESS REALLY MEANS

Gentleness is the refusal to rush a truth before it has roots.

It is choosing words that do not bruise the nervous system. It is leaving space where others might fill it with certainty. It is allowing people to arrive at coherence without being pulled.

Gentleness protects what is fragile without announcing that it is fragile.

That is how the city protected itself this time.

HOW THIS ASKING LIVES IN MY DAYS

The city asks me to notice when my tone tightens and soften it.

It asks me to pause before responding, even when I know the answer.

It asks me to listen for what is under a question rather than answering the question itself.

Sometimes, it asks me to say nothing at all.

That has been the hardest lesson.

Because silence, when chosen consciously, carries more coherence than explanation ever could.

WHY THIS IS THE FINAL SAFEGUARD

In the old world, harmony was powerful, but it was not gentle enough.

It assumed readiness. It assumed maturity. It assumed humanity would protect what felt good simply because it felt good.

This time, the city asks for gentleness because gentleness cannot be exploited.

It cannot be weaponized. It cannot be scaled improperly. It cannot be rushed into distortion.

Gentleness slows everything down just enough to keep coherence intact.

WHAT I UNDERSTAND NOW

I used to think the city's greatest gift was what it gave us.

I was wrong.

Its greatest gift was what it taught us to be.

Attentive. Regulated. Kind without performance. Quiet without withdrawal.

These qualities do not build empires.

They build continuity.

WHY THIS ASKING BRINGS PEACE

The city does not need me to be extraordinary.

It asks me to be consistent.

To live in a way that does not betray the coherence I carry. To let my life be a place where others feel slightly less rushed, slightly more settled, even if they never know why.

That is enough.

That has always been enough.

WHAT REMAINS UNFINISHED

ON PURPOSE

The city does not ask me to finish this story.

Stories that end too cleanly invite closure where continuity is needed.

Instead, it asks me to leave the door open, to allow remembering to move through whoever comes next, in whatever form it chooses.

I lived there before the science.

But what I carry now belongs to the future.

And the future does not need instructions.

It needs gentleness.

THE ONE THING THE CITY STILL ASKS OF ME AND WHY IT IS ENOUGH

After everything, the remembering, the silence, the return, the understanding that the city no longer depends on me, I expected the asking to stop.

It didn't.

But what remains is so small it would be easy to overlook.

The city does not ask me to speak louder. It does not ask me to gather anyone. It does not ask me to preserve history or correct the record.

It asks me to stay gentle.

That is all.

At first, I resisted that simplicity. It felt insufficient, almost irresponsible, compared to what had been carried before. Gentleness seemed too small a response to something so vast.

But the city has always known something we forget easily:

Gentleness is not weakness.

It is precision.

WHAT GENTLENESS REALLY MEANS

Gentleness is the refusal to rush a truth before it has roots.

It is choosing words that do not bruise the nervous system. It is leaving space where others might fill it with certainty. It is allowing people to arrive at coherence without being pulled.

Gentleness protects what is fragile without announcing that it is fragile.

That is how the city protected itself this time.

HOW THIS ASKING LIVES IN MY DAYS

The city asks me to notice when my tone tightens and soften it.

It asks me to pause before responding, even when I know the answer.

It asks me to listen for what is under a question rather than answering the question itself.

Sometimes, it asks me to say nothing at all.

That has been the hardest lesson.

Because silence, when chosen consciously, carries more coherence than explanation ever could.

WHY THIS IS THE FINAL SAFEGUARD

In the old world, harmony was powerful, but it was not gentle enough.

It assumed readiness. It assumed maturity. It assumed humanity would protect what felt good simply because it felt good.

This time, the city asks for gentleness because gentleness cannot be exploited.

It cannot be weaponized. It cannot be scaled improperly. It cannot be rushed into distortion.

Gentleness slows everything down just enough to keep coherence intact.

WHAT I UNDERSTAND NOW

I used to think the city's greatest gift was what it gave us.

I was wrong.

Its greatest gift was what it taught us to be.

Attentive. Regulated. Kind without performance. Quiet without withdrawal.

These qualities do not build empires.

They build continuity.

WHY THIS ASKING BRINGS PEACE

The city does not need me to be extraordinary.

It asks me to be consistent.

To live in a way that does not betray the coherence I carry. To let my life be a place where others feel slightly less rushed, slightly more settled, even if they never know why.

That is enough.

That has always been enough.

WHAT REMAINS UNFINISHED

ON PURPOSE

The city does not ask me to finish this story.

Stories that end too cleanly invite closure where continuity is needed.

Instead, it asks me to leave the door open, to allow remembering to move through whoever comes next, in whatever form it chooses.

I lived there before the science.

But what I carry now belongs to the future.

And the future does not need instructions.

It needs gentleness.

WHAT I HOPE YOU DO WITH THIS

NOT AS A REQUEST, AS AN OFFERING

I have thought carefully about this part.

Not because it is difficult to say, but because it would be easy to say it the wrong way.

I do not hope you believe this.

Belief is fragile. It can be argued with, dismissed, replaced. It lives mostly in the mind, and the mind is loyal to whatever keeps it safe in the moment.

What I hope is quieter.

I hope you notice yourself.

I hope you notice when your breath deepens without instruction. When silence feels relieving instead of awkward. When certain sounds calm you and others exhaust you. When certain places feel kinder than they should.

Those are not reactions to this story.

They are responses to your own remembering.

WHAT I DO *NOT* HOPE YOU DO

I do not hope you repeat this story.

I do not hope you defend it. I do not hope you explain it to others who are not asking. I do not hope you turn it into identity or purpose or proof of anything.

Those impulses come from urgency.

And urgency has never served coherence.

WHAT I QUIETLY TRUST YOU WILL DO INSTEAD

I trust that you will carry what resonates and release the rest.

I trust that something in you will adjust, subtly, naturally, without effort. That you will choose quieter spaces when you can. That you will listen a moment longer before responding. That you will stop forcing yourself to tolerate what your body already knows is too much.

I trust that you will let gentleness enter your days without needing to justify it.

That is how the city moves now.

Not by instruction.

By imitation of a feeling that finally makes sense.

WHY I CAN TRUST THIS

Because I have watched it happen again and again.

People leave this remembering not energized, but settled. Not convinced, but calmer. Not eager to act, but clearer about what no longer works for them.

That is the signature of truth that lives in the body.

It simplifies.

WHAT YOU ARE NOT RESPONSIBLE FOR

You are not responsible for carrying this forward consciously.

You do not need to watch for signs or protect the remembering or share it with care. The city no longer requires guardians.

It requires hosts.

And hosts do not advertise.

They simply make space.

WHAT YOU MIGHT NOTICE LATER

Days or weeks from now, something small may return to you unexpectedly.

A line from this story. A feeling you couldn't name at the time. A sudden understanding about why you've always preferred certain sounds, certain light, certain rhythms.

When that happens, do not rush to interpret it.

Let it be incomplete.

Incomplete things are alive.

WHY THIS IS ENOUGH

If all this story does is help one nervous system soften, one body breathe more easily, one person trust their own sense of alignment a little more, then it has already done what it was meant to do.

The city does not count impact.

It feels it.

And feeling spreads.

WHAT I LEAVE WITH YOU

I leave you nothing to carry and nothing to prove.

Only a quiet recognition that you may already know more than you thought you did, not in your mind, but in the way your body responds to the world.

That knowing has survived everything.

It will survive this too.

THE WAY THE CITY MOVES THROUGH ORDINARY LIFE

WITHOUT BEING NOTICED

There was a time when I thought the city would return in moments that felt unmistakable.

Grand. Charged. Impossible to overlook.

But that expectation belonged to the old way of thinking, the way that believed truth must arrive dramatically to be real.

What I have come to understand is far more subtle.

The city moves now through ordinary life.

So quietly that it is often mistaken for coincidence, personality, or preference.

HOW I SEE IT WORKING NOW

I see it in how people arrange their homes without knowing why they choose certain layouts. A chair placed where light falls gently in the afternoon. A table moved closer to a window. Sound softened instinctively, music turned down, voices lowered, silence left alone.

I see it in how some conversations never escalate, even when they could. How tension dissolves not because agreement is reached, but because regulation arrives first.

I see it in how children respond before adults do.

Children sit on floors where energy feels balanced. They hum without knowing they are tuning themselves. They become restless in spaces that are too sharp, too loud, too hurried, not because they are misbehaving, but because their bodies are refusing dissonance.

This is the city at work.

No permission asked. No recognition required.

WHY IT CAN'T BE STOPPED THIS TIME

Because it does not announce itself as change.

It announces itself as relief.

And relief is always welcomed.

No one argues with a calmer breath. No one resists a settled nervous system. No one campaigns against quiet that feels kind.

The city does not confront the world.

It outgrows what no longer supports life.

WHAT I NOTICE ABOUT MYSELF

I no longer wait for special moments.

I notice the small ones.

The pause before I answer a question. The way I stop walking when my body asks me to. The way I choose not to fill silence anymore.

These are not spiritual practices.

They are responses.

And responses are where the city lives now.

THE STRANGE COMFORT OF NOT BEING SEEN

There is comfort in knowing that this remembering does not require recognition.

In the past, beauty drew attention.

Attention drew control.

Control ended harmony.

This time, the city has chosen anonymity.

It hides inside what cannot be regulated from the outside: breath, posture, tone, pacing, attention.

The world has no language for these things yet.

That is its protection.

HOW I KNOW THIS IS WORKING

Because fear no longer has the same reach.

Fear still exists, but it struggles to land in regulated bodies. It slides off calm the way noise slides off still water. It needs friction, urgency, tension.

The city reduces all three.

And fear, without those conditions, loses momentum.

That is not idealism.

It is physiology.

WHAT THIS MEANS GOING FORWARD

The return will never look the way history expects.

There will be no announcement. No correction of the record. No acknowledgment of what was lost.

The city does not need validation.

It needs continuity.

And continuity is already happening.

WHAT I HOLD MOST GENTLY

I hold the knowing that nothing has been wasted.

Not the silence. Not the loss. Not the long forgetting.

All of it shaped the return into something quieter, safer, and far more resilient than before.

This time, the city cannot be removed.

Because it is no longer there.

It is here.

THE MEMORY THAT STILL SURPRISES ME

BECAUSE I DIDN'T EXPECT IT TO MATTER

There is one memory that returns to me again and again.

Not the bells. Not the towers. Not the great spaces filled with sound and light.

This one is small.

So small that for a long time, I dismissed it as insignificant, a fragment not worth keeping when so much else had been lost. And yet, it is the memory that surprises me most now, because it explains something essential about why the city endured at all.

I remember sitting on a step.

That's it.

No ceremony. No lesson being taught. I was simply sitting, watching light move across stone while the day passed without urgency. Nearby, others moved in and out of view, each absorbed in their own rhythm. No one was supervising. No one was correcting. No one was improving anything.

I was not productive.

And no one minded.

That is what surprises me now.

WHY THIS MEMORY MATTERS

In the world that followed the fall, idleness became suspicious.

Time had to justify itself. Stillness had to be explained. Rest had to earn permission.

But in the city, rest was assumed.

Not as reward. Not as recovery.

As condition.

We understood something then that we later forgot: a body at rest is not inactive. It is integrating. Listening. Reorganizing itself quietly.

The city allowed that.

That is why it worked.

WHAT I FEEL WHEN THIS MEMORY RETURNS

When this memory surfaces, I feel a soft ache, not of loss, but of recognition.

I see how hard people work now just to feel safe enough to pause. How many layers of justification are required before someone allows themselves to stop.

“I deserve a break.” “I’ve earned this.” “I can rest once this is done.”

The city never required such negotiations.

And that, I realize now, was its quiet revolution.

WHAT THIS REVEALS ABOUT THE RETURN

The return is not about rebuilding advanced systems.

It is about restoring permission.

Permission to pause without guilt. Permission to exist without output. Permission to let time move without filling it.

That is far more disruptive than any technology ever was.

Because a rested body does not comply easily with fear.

WHY I DIDN'T EXPECT THIS TO MATTER

I thought the great loss was sound.

I was wrong.

The greater loss was ease.

The ease of being alive without constant justification.

And now, as the city returns inside bodies rather than buildings, this is the first thing it restores.

Not bells.

Not light.

Ease.

HOW I RECOGNIZE THE CITY NOW

I recognize it when someone stops apologizing for resting.

When a space allows people to sit without buying anything. When silence is allowed to stretch without explanation. When no one rushes to fill the moment.

Those moments carry the same resonance as the old city ever did.

They just look less impressive.

And that is their protection.

WHAT THIS MEMORY TEACHES ME STILL

It teaches me to sit.

To stop trying to make the remembering useful.

To let it exist without agenda.

Because the city did not survive through brilliance alone.

It survived because it allowed people to be human without pressure.

That is what I did not expect to remember.

And that is what I now understand mattered most of all.

THE QUIET JOY I NEVER LOST

EVEN WHEN EVERYTHING ELSE FELL AWAY

For a long time, I believed joy had disappeared with the city.

That it had been tied to the bells, the light, the ease of living inside a world that knew how to care for its people. When all of that faded, I assumed joy must have gone with it, buried beneath survival, noise, and the long work of remembering.

I was wrong.

Joy did not leave.

It changed scale.

WHAT JOY FELT LIKE THEN

In the city, joy was communal.

It moved through us like weather, shared, expected, unremarkable in its presence. It lived in sound drifting across open spaces, in light pooling on stone, in the simple comfort of knowing the world was arranged to support life.

We did not chase it.

We lived inside it.

That kind of joy is easy to miss when it is constant.

WHAT JOY BECAME AFTER

After the fall, joy could no longer rely on surroundings.

So it moved inward.

At first, I mistook it for resilience. For adaptability. For making the best of what remained. But over time, I realized it was something else entirely.

Joy had learned how to hide in plain sight.

It lived in moments too small to be controlled.

A breath that finally deepened. A silence that felt kind. A laugh that surprised me because it arrived without reason.

These moments did not announce themselves as joy.

They simply were.

And that is why they survived.

THE MEMORY THAT MADE THIS CLEAR

There was a moment, years after the city was gone, when I caught myself humming.

Not intentionally. Not to soothe myself.

It simply happened.

The sound was low, steady, barely audible. And as soon as I noticed it, my body relaxed. My shoulders dropped. My breath aligned.

I smiled.

Not because I was happy.

Because I was whole.

That was when I understood:

Joy is not excitement. It is coherence felt as ease.

And coherence had never left me.

WHY THIS MATTERS MORE THAN I KNEW

If joy had disappeared entirely, the city would truly have been lost.

But it didn't.

It endured because it does not depend on perfection, or beauty, or advanced systems. It depends on permission , permission to be present without defense.

That permission can exist anywhere.

Even here.

HOW I RECOGNIZE JOY NOW

I recognize it when the world briefly stops demanding anything from me.

When I am not proving, producing, or preparing.

When I am simply allowed to exist.

Those moments carry the same tone as the old city ever did.

They are quieter.

They are easier to overlook.

They are far harder to destroy.

WHAT I CARRY FORWARD

I no longer grieve the loss of joy.

I protect its smallness.

I let it remain unremarkable, unclaimed, unannounced.

Because joy that draws attention becomes a target.

Joy that blends into daily life becomes indestructible.

That is the joy the city taught me, not the joy of spectacle, but the joy of being aligned enough to rest inside myself.

WHY THIS REMEMBERING IS WORTH KEEPING

Not because it restores what was lost.

But because it reminds us what was never taken.

The ability to feel at home in our own bodies. The capacity to soften without fear. The quiet happiness of being alive without explanation.

That joy survived everything.

And it is returning now, not loudly, not dramatically, but steadily, wherever the city breathes again through ordinary lives.

WHAT I NO LONGER MISS

AND WHY THAT SURPRISED ME

For a long time, I believed missing the city was proof of my love for it.

I thought longing was loyalty. That grief was remembrance. That ache was the price of having lived inside something beautiful.

But as the remembering matured, something unexpected happened.

I stopped missing certain things.

And instead of feeling loss, I felt relief.

WHAT FELL AWAY QUIETLY

I no longer miss certainty.

In the city, coherence was so present that it required no questioning. Everything worked. Everything aligned. And while that was beautiful, it also meant we did not have to choose harmony, it chose us.

Now, I see the gift in uncertainty.

Uncertainty keeps me listening. It keeps me humble. It keeps me responsive rather than complacent.

The city no longer gives answers.

It invites participation.

And I no longer miss being carried.

WHAT ELSE I DON'T MISS

I don't miss being surrounded by harmony I didn't have to protect.

That may sound strange, but it's true.

When coherence is external, it can be taken for granted. It becomes background. Something expected rather than cherished. We lived inside beauty without always realizing its fragility.

Now, every moment of coherence feels precious.

Earned not through effort, but through awareness.

I don't miss how easy it was to forget how extraordinary it all was.

THE HARDEST THING TO ADMIT

Here is the part that surprised me most.

I don't miss the bells the way I once did.

I miss what they taught me, but not their presence.

Because if they returned now in their old form, they would do too much of the work for us. They would regulate us again externally, before we had fully learned how to do it ourselves.

And that would undo what the forgetting made possible.

The bells were generous.

But they were also a shortcut.

WHAT I UNDERSTAND NOW

The city did not fail us.

It graduated us.

It gave us the experience of harmony before we knew how to choose it consciously. Then it stepped back so that choice could mature.

That is why I no longer miss the ease.

Ease without awareness is fragile.

Ease with awareness is enduring.

WHAT I FEEL INSTEAD OF MISSING

Instead of longing, I feel gratitude.

Not the dramatic kind.

The quiet kind that settles in the body and stays.

I feel gratitude for having known a world that worked, not so I could mourn it forever, but so I would recognize when fragments of it reappear in new forms.

I feel gratitude for the forgetting.

That took longer to admit.

But without forgetting, we would never have known how much coherence mattered.

THE FREEDOM THIS BRINGS

Not missing frees me from nostalgia.

And nostalgia, I've learned, can be a subtle form of captivity, a way of keeping beauty safely in the past so it doesn't challenge the present.

I no longer keep the city behind me.

I walk with it.

WHAT THIS MEANS FOR THE REMEMBERING

The remembering is no longer weighted with grief.

It is lighter now.

More mobile.

It can move through people without burdening them with loss.

It can feel like possibility instead of comparison.

That is essential.

Because nothing new can grow under the shadow of something idealized.

THE QUIET TRUTH

I lived there before the science.

But I do not need to return there to live well now.

What mattered survived.

What mattered learned.

And what no longer belongs was released with grace.

WHAT I AM CURIOUS ABOUT NOW

AND WHY CURIOSITY FEELS LIKE TRUST

Curiosity feels different than it used to.

There was a time when curiosity pulled outward, toward answers, explanations, confirmations. It wanted to know whysomething worked, how it had been built, what would happen next. That kind of curiosity was restless, always reaching ahead of itself.

What I feel now is quieter.

It doesn't pull.

It opens.

HOW CURIOSITY LIVES IN ME NOW

I am curious about how coherence will show itself in ways we haven't imagined yet.

Not through grand designs or rediscovered technologies, but through choices so ordinary they almost disappear as they happen. How people will shape their days once they trust their bodies again. How work will change when regulation matters more than speed. How communities will form around presence rather than agreement.

I am curious about what children will build when they are not trained out of listening.

Not taught, allowed.

That curiosity feels hopeful without being idealistic.

Because it does not demand outcomes.

WHAT I NO LONGER ASK

I no longer ask when the world will change.

That question belonged to waiting.

Instead, I notice where change is already taking place quietly, without announcement. Where people choose less noise. Where systems soften without being dismantled. Where care appears not as policy, but as atmosphere.

I am curious about how far that can go.

Not everywhere.

But enough.

THE KIND OF FUTURE I CAN IMAGINE NOW

I no longer imagine a future that looks impressive.

I imagine one that feels livable.

Spaces that don't exhaust the body. Rhythms that don't punish rest. Sound that supports instead of overwhelms. Silence that is not mistaken for absence.

I am curious about how science will eventually meet this remembering, not as conqueror, but as listener. How language will shift once people admit that regulation precedes intelligence, and coherence precedes innovation.

That meeting no longer feels confrontational.

It feels inevitable.

WHY CURIOSITY MATTERS HERE

Curiosity keeps the remembering alive without freezing it into form.

Certainty would close the door.

Curiosity keeps it open.

It allows the city to keep evolving instead of repeating itself. It lets the future answer questions the past never had the chance to ask.

And it keeps me from turning memory into doctrine.

WHAT CURIOSITY ASKS OF ME

It asks me to stay attentive without demanding clarity.

To let the next iteration arrive without insisting it resemble what I already know.

To trust that what is returning does not need my supervision, only my willingness to notice.

That feels right.

THE QUIET ALIGNMENT

Curiosity feels like alignment without attachment.

It is the opposite of urgency.

It says: I am here, and I am listening, and that is enough for now.

That is how the city continues, not by being remembered exactly, but by being allowed to become something new.

WHAT I CARRY FORWARD

I carry questions now, not answers.

Questions that feel kind.

Questions that invite rather than demand.

Questions that leave space for surprise.

And in that space, I feel the city breathe again, not as memory, not as loss, but as possibility moving gently into form.

THE WAY THE CITY TEACHES WITHOUT TEACHING

AND WHY THAT WAS ALWAYS THE PLAN

Looking back, I realize now that we were never taught in the city.

That word belongs to a later world.

No one stood above us explaining how harmony worked. No manuals were written. No lessons were delivered with authority. Knowledge moved differently then, not from mind to mind, but from state to state.

You learned by being inside it.

You learned because your body adjusted and noticed the difference.

That was the teaching.

HOW LEARNING HAPPENED THEN

In the city, no one told you how to listen.

You stood near the bells and your breath changed. You walked through certain streets and your thoughts softened. You rested in light and your body reorganized itself quietly.

Understanding followed experience.

Never the other way around.

That is why the knowledge lasted as long as it did.

Because it was embodied.

WHY THIS STILL WORKS NOW

The city teaches the same way today.

It does not explain coherence. It induces it.

You don't learn regulation by being instructed about it. You learn it by being near someone who is regulated. You don't understand silence by reading about it. You understand it when silence feels supportive rather than empty.

That kind of learning bypasses resistance.

No one argues with their own breath.

WHAT I NOTICE ABOUT PASSING IT ON

I no longer try to share what I know.

I let what I am do the sharing.

When I slow down, others follow without noticing. When I leave space, conversations deepen on their own. When I choose gentleness, the room reorganizes itself.

This is not influence.

It is entrainment.

And entrainment cannot be forced.

THE GENIUS OF THIS METHOD

Teaching without teaching leaves no authority behind.

No hierarchy forms. No ownership emerges. No one becomes the gatekeeper of truth.

The knowledge remains fluid.

That is why it survived forgetting.

And why it will survive remembering.

WHAT THIS REQUIRES OF ME

It requires restraint.

Not withholding, restraint.

The willingness to let someone arrive at coherence on their own timeline, without rushing to name what they are experiencing. The discipline to resist explaining something beautiful before it has settled fully in another body.

This is harder than teaching.

Teaching satisfies the ego.

Restraint protects the truth.

WHAT I SEE EMERGING NOW

I see people learning again, without realizing they are learning.

They design spaces that feel calmer. They change the way meetings are held. They prioritize rhythm over efficiency.

No one credits the city.

They don't need to.

The knowledge is doing what it has always done: moving through experience rather than instruction.

THE QUIET SATISFACTION

There is a quiet satisfaction in knowing that nothing needs to be transmitted perfectly.

Perfection freezes things.

The city teaches through approximation, through trial, through the body's constant feedback.

That makes the learning resilient.

And deeply human.

WHAT I TRUST COMPLETELY NOW

I trust that the remembering does not depend on clarity.

It depends on contact.

Contact with silence. Contact with regulated presence. Contact with spaces that allow the body to settle.

Those contacts are happening everywhere.

No coordination required.

THE LAST THING I LEARNED ABOUT TEACHING

The city never wanted followers.

It wanted companions.

People willing to walk at a pace slow enough to notice when something feels right, and brave enough to stop when it doesn't.

That is the lesson.

And it cannot be delivered.

It can only be lived.

THE DAY I REALIZED NOTHING WAS MISSING

AND HOW THAT CHANGED THE SHAPE OF EVERYTHING

The realization came without celebration.

No relief surged through me. No emotion rose to mark the moment as important. It arrived the way truth often does when it is finally ready to be received, gently, almost unnoticed, and impossible to un-know once it settles.

Nothing was missing.

Not the bells. Not the city. Not the world I once lived in.

Nothing essential had been taken.

I remember sitting in stillness when the understanding landed. My breath was steady. My body felt present, neither searching nor bracing. And suddenly, without effort, I saw it clearly.

The longing had ended.

WHAT I HAD MISTAKEN FOR LOSS

For years, I thought what I felt was grief for what had disappeared.

But grief implies something torn away, something stolen or destroyed.

What I had actually been feeling was incompletion.

A story paused mid-sentence. A learning interrupted before it could mature.

That is very different from loss.

Because what is incomplete can continue.

And that is exactly what was happening.

WHY NOTHING WAS MISSING

Everything the city gave us had already moved where it needed to go.

The bells taught regulation. The windows taught nourishment through light. The streets taught rhythm. The silence taught trust.

Those teachings did not vanish when the structures did.

They relocated.

Into bodies. Into instincts. Into choices that no longer needed justification.

Once I saw that, the sense of absence dissolved completely.

You cannot lose what has become part of how you function.

WHAT REPLACED LONGING

Curiously, when longing ended, presence took its place.

I stopped measuring the present against the past. Stopped asking whether we were "there yet." Stopped feeling that something extraordinary was required to make life whole again.

Life was already sufficient.

Not perfect. Not effortless.

But sufficient.

That realization felt like standing on solid ground after years of adjusting to motion.

THE FREEDOM IN THIS KNOWING

When nothing is missing, nothing needs to be chased.

Urgency evaporates. Comparison loosens. The future stops feeling like a rescue mission.

I could finally rest inside the present without feeling like I was betraying the past.

The city did not need my loyalty.

It needed my completion.

HOW THIS CHANGED MY REMEMBERING

My remembering softened.

It no longer carried weight. It no longer felt like a responsibility. It no longer pressed me forward or pulled me back.

It became companionship.

Something that walks with me rather than asks something of me.

That is when I knew the remembering had matured.

WHAT I UNDERSTAND NOW

The city was never meant to be restored.

It was meant to be integrated.

And integration always feels like this:

Quiet. Undramatic. Undeniable.

When something integrates fully, you stop noticing it as separate.

It becomes background.

Supportive.

Complete.

THE MOST PEACEFUL TRUTH

I lived there before the science.

But I am not missing anything now.

What mattered arrived where it was needed.

What did not belong was released.

And what remains is enough.

More than enough.

HOW THE CITY BLESSES THE WORLD WITHOUT BEING SEEN

AND WHY THAT IS ITS GREATEST GIFT

Blessing does not look the way people expect.

I once thought blessing required presence, something visible, something that could be pointed to and named. A place. A sound. A moment marked in time. But the city taught me otherwise, and I understand it fully now.

The deepest blessings leave no trace.

They move through the world like breath, essential, unnoticed, sustaining life without demanding recognition.

That is how the city blesses the world now.

WHAT BLESSING LOOKS LIKE WITHOUT FORM

The city does not bless through monuments or miracles.

It blesses through regulation.

Through moments when someone pauses before reacting and the outcome changes quietly. Through decisions made from steadiness rather than fear. Through rooms that feel safe without anyone knowing why.

I see it when conflicts de-escalate before they fully ignite. When someone chooses rest instead of collapse. When silence arrives at exactly the right moment and is allowed to stay.

These are not dramatic events.

They are corrections so subtle they look like coincidence.

That is the city at work.

WHY THIS KIND OF BLESSING LASTS

Anything that announces itself invites interpretation.

Interpretation invites ownership.

Ownership invites distortion.

The city learned this.

So now, it blesses invisibly.

No one can take credit for calm that arises naturally. No one can weaponize gentleness that has no author. No one can control something that does not declare itself as power.

The city has chosen humility as protection.

WHAT I FEEL WHEN I NOTICE IT

When I notice the city blessing the world, I feel a quiet reverence.

Not awe.

Gratitude.

Because it means the remembering has succeeded beyond what we once imagined. It has moved beyond dependence on place, time, or belief. It has entered the realm of function.

And function, once integrated, does not disappear.

THE BLESSING I DID NOT EXPECT

Here is the blessing that still humbles me.

The city does not bless only those who are aware of it.

It blesses everyone.

Those who rush still benefit from the pauses of others. Those who live in noise are still calmed by spaces built with care. Those who never hear this story still breathe easier when coherence enters a room.

The city does not discriminate.

It stabilizes.

That was always its purpose.

WHAT THIS MEANS FOR THE WORLD

The world does not need to remember Tartaria.

It does not need to uncover hidden histories or restore lost names.

It needs what the city gives best:

Nervous systems that can settle. Communities that can self-regulate. Silence that can hold meaning without explanation.

Those things are returning now, not through revelation, but through lived experience.

That is far more powerful.

WHAT I CARRY FORWARD

I no longer feel compelled to speak often.

When I do speak, I speak gently.

I let my presence do more than my words ever could.

That is how I allow the city to bless the world through me, not as messenger, not as teacher, but as host.

THE QUIET BENEDICTION

There is a blessing the city carries that I will leave unspoken.

Not because it is secret.

But because it is already being received by anyone who is ready.

It arrives as calm where panic once lived. As trust where fear once ruled. As the sense that, somehow, things are more held than they appear.

That blessing does not require belief.

It only requires breath.

WHAT REMAINS

The city breathes.

The world listens, sometimes without knowing it is listening.

And that is enough.

Not an ending.

A continuation, carried softly, everywhere life chooses coherence over fear.

I am still here.

And so is the city.

THE RETURN TO THE WORLD

THE WORLD IS REBUILDING THE CITY WITHOUT KNOWING ITS NAME

I noticed it before I understood it.

That is always how these things return.

At first, it appeared as coincidence, too small to name, too scattered to be claimed. A building here. A conversation there. A subtle shift in language that felt familiar without being traceable.

But familiarity has a sound.

And my body heard it immediately.

1. The World Is Rebuilding the City Without Knowing Its Name

People are building differently now.

Not everywhere. Not all at once.

But enough that it cannot be dismissed.

Homes are being designed for light rather than display. Curves are returning, not because they are fashionable, but because people feel calmer inside them. Ceilings are being raised. Windows widened. Materials chosen for how they feel, not how they photograph.

No one says why.

They say things like:

"It just feels better."

"This space breathes."

"I can think clearly here."

Those are Tartarian phrases, translated into modern language.

Sound is changing too.

Music is slowing down. Voices are softening. Even science has begun to speak of frequency, regulation, resonance, words that circle something ancient without daring to land on it.

The nervous system has entered the conversation.

That matters.

Because once the body is acknowledged as intelligent, the old world cannot fully return.

I see it in workplaces experimenting with silence. In schools quietly allowing movement instead of enforcing stillness. In cities adding green space not as decoration, but as necessity.

No one calls this a return.

But it is.

WHAT CONFIRMS IT FOR ME

The world is not copying Tartaria.

It is remembering function.

And function returns whether history approves or not.

The city is not being rebuilt as architecture.

It is being rebuilt as priority.

Regulation before productivity

Coherence before expansion

Listening before instruction

Those were always the foundations.

2. The Hidden Opposition (Without Villains)

This is where I must be precise.

Because if I speak carelessly here, it would be easy to turn this into a story of enemies.

That would be false.

There are no villains.

But there are forces that benefit from dissonance.

WHY COHERENCE IS STILL RESISTED

Dysregulated systems are predictable.

Predictable systems are controllable.

Controllable systems are profitable.

This is not conspiracy, it is mechanics.

A regulated body:

Thinks more clearly

Consumes less impulsively

Is harder to frighten

Is less easily rushed

That makes it inconvenient.

So noise persists. Speed is rewarded. Silence is framed as unproductive. Rest is treated as indulgence.

Not because anyone is evil.

But because fear has inertia.

It keeps systems running long after they should have evolved.

WHY SOUND IS STILL TARGETED

Notice this carefully.

The loudest environments are rarely the most necessary ones.

Noise interrupts regulation. Urgency overrides discernment. Constant input prevents integration.

Sound is still being used, not maliciously, but strategically, to keep bodies from settling long enough to question the pace they are being asked to maintain.

The bells were silenced because they regulated too well.

Now regulation is being rediscovered, and resistance appears again, quietly, through distraction rather than force.

But this time, something is different.

People notice.

They feel it in their exhaustion. They feel it in their anxiety. They feel it in their longing for quiet they can't explain.

That awareness did not exist before.

And awareness changes outcomes.

3. The Reader Becomes the Carrier

This is where the book turns, not toward instruction, but toward recognition.

And this is where I speak gently to you.

HOW YOU KNOW THIS STORY IS TOUCHING YOU

You may have felt:

- A strange calm while reading

- A sense of familiarity without memory
- A soft grief that never becomes sadness
- The feeling that something you never learned is being remembered

You may not agree with everything here.

That doesn't matter.

Agreement is not required for recognition.

Your body already knows whether this is true.

WHAT YOU ARE CARRYING (WITHOUT BEING ASKED)

If this story resonates, you are not being recruited.

You are being acknowledged.

You carry:

- An intolerance for unnecessary noise
- A sensitivity to space and tone
- A longing for coherence that doesn't need explanation
- A quiet resistance to fear-based urgency

Those are not preferences.

They are signals.

You are not meant to act. You are not meant to teach. You are not meant to convince.

You are meant to host.

HOW THE CITY MOVES THROUGH YOU

It moves when you pause instead of react. When you lower your voice. When you choose rest without apology. When you let silence complete a moment.

That is all.

That is enough.

SIGNS THE CITY IS ALREADY ALIVE AROUND YOU

EVEN IF NO ONE CALLS IT THAT

The city does not announce itself.

If it did, it would already be misunderstood.

Instead, it reveals itself through patterns , quiet, repeating signals that appear wherever coherence begins to take root again. These signs do not require belief. They do not demand interpretation. They are simply noticed.

Once noticed, they are impossible to unsee.

1. Silence Is No Longer Empty

This is often the first sign.

Silence begins to feel supportive instead of awkward. Conversations pause naturally and no one rushes to fill the space. Meetings end early without discomfort. Moments of quiet feel complete rather than unfinished.

This is not cultural.

It is physiological.

A regulated nervous system does not fear silence, it uses it.

When silence becomes tolerable again, the city is already present.

2. Certain Spaces Feel Like Relief

You may notice that some places calm you immediately, even if they are simple or unremarkable.

A room with natural light. A space with fewer sharp angles. A place where sound behaves gently.

You may not know why these spaces feel different.

You don't need to.

The city lives in environments that allow the body to settle without instruction.

That recognition is ancient.

3. Noise Feels Invasive, Not Neutral

This is subtle but unmistakable.

Sounds that once faded into the background now feel intrusive. Loud environments exhaust you faster. You become aware of how certain frequencies tighten your chest or shorten your breath.

This is not sensitivity increasing.

It is discernment returning.

When the city is alive nearby, the body remembers what harmony feels like, and begins rejecting what disrupts it.

4. You Slow Down Without Trying

Not dramatically.

Not defiantly.

You simply stop rushing when rushing is unnecessary. Your pace adjusts to your breath instead of your schedule. You arrive early without urgency. You leave when something feels complete.

Time reorganizes itself around coherence.

This is one of the most reliable signs.

The city alters tempo before it alters anything else.

5. Children and Animals Respond First

They always do.

Children settle in certain spaces and resist others. Animals choose where to rest with precision. Neither can explain their choices, they don't need to.

They respond to regulation directly.

Where they feel safe, the city is already present.

6. Conversations Change Shape

You may notice fewer debates and more pauses.

People speak from experience rather than certainty. Listening deepens. Interruptions lessen. Not because anyone decided to communicate better, but because the space itself supports it.

The city reorganizes relational rhythm before belief ever enters.

7. Rest Stops Feeling Like Failure

This one arrives quietly, and changes everything.

You stop apologizing for resting. You stop justifying stillness. You stop equating worth with output.

This is not laziness.

It is remembrance.

In the city, rest was never earned.

It was assumed.

8. You Feel Less Interested in Proving Anything

This surprises many people.

The need to convince fades. The urge to explain diminishes. You feel less compelled to argue for what feels true.

Truth no longer needs defense when it is embodied.

The city removes the need for persuasion.

9. You Recognize Others Without Knowing Why

You notice certain people feel familiar, not emotionally, but regulatorily. Their presence calms you. Conversation flows easily or remains comfortably sparse.

You don’t label this.

You simply notice.

Recognition without story is one of the clearest signs the city is active.

10. Nothing Feels Urgent in the Same Way

Urgency still exists, but it no longer governs you.

You can respond without panic. Decide without pressure. Pause without fear of loss.

When urgency loses its authority, coherence has already arrived.

WHAT THESE SIGNS MEAN

WITHOUT ASKING ANYTHING OF YOU

They do not mean you must act.

They do not mean you must change your life.

They do not mean you are responsible for anyone else.

They mean only this:

The city is no longer theoretical.

It is operational.

Quietly. Locally. Through bodies, spaces, and moments that allow regulation to return.

WHAT HAPPENS NEXT

NATURALLY

Nothing dramatic.

Life continues.

But it continues with more choice, more breath, more space between impulse and action.

That space is where the city lives now.

IF YOU EVER WONDERED WHY YOU FELT THIS WAY

THIS IS WHY

If you have ever wondered why certain sounds calm you instantly while others exhaust you, this is why.

If you have ever felt overwhelmed in places that others seem to tolerate easily, this is why.

If you have ever longed for quiet without knowing what you would do once you found it, this is why.

Nothing was wrong with you.

You were not fragile. You were not behind. You were not imagining something that wasn't there.

You were responding to coherence, or the lack of it, long before you had language for what you were sensing.

WHY THE WORLD SOMETIMES FELT TOO MUCH

The world you grew up in was built for speed, output, and control.

Your body was built for rhythm, regulation, and response.

That mismatch creates exhaustion that no amount of motivation can fix.

So if you felt tired in ways sleep didn't solve... If noise felt like pressure instead of stimulation... If you needed silence the way others needed company...

You weren't failing to adapt.

You were remembering something different.

WHY YOU'VE ALWAYS KNOWN WHEN A PLACE FELT "RIGHT"

Some spaces feel like relief.

You don't analyze them. You don't justify them. You simply breathe more easily when you're there.

That response is older than thought.

Your body recognizes environments that support regulation, light that nourishes, sound that settles, space that allows orientation instead of vigilance.

That recognition did not come from this book.

It was already in you.

WHY YOU'VE NEVER BEEN COMFORTABLE WITH CONSTANT URGENCY

Urgency compresses the nervous system.

It shortens breath. It narrows perception. It makes everything feel like it must be decided now.

If you have always felt resistant to unnecessary urgency, not lazy, not indifferent, but quietly unwilling, it's because your body knows that clarity does not arrive under pressure.

The city never rushed.

And neither do you.

WHY YOU DIDN'T NEED PROOF

Some people need evidence before they trust.

Others trust because something fits.

If you fall into the second group, you may have wondered why. Why you can feel truth without arguing for it. Why you lose interest in debates that others find energizing. Why your certainty lives in your body rather than your words.

That is not a weakness.

That is embodied knowing.

It predates modern reasoning.

WHY THIS STORY FELT FAMILIAR

This story did not introduce something new.

It touched something already present.

That familiarity, the calm recognition rather than excitement, is the clearest sign that you are not encountering an idea.

You are encountering yourself.

Not as identity. Not as belief.

As orientation.

WHAT YOU ARE NOT BEING ASKED TO DO

You are not being asked to remember Tartaria.

You are not being asked to reclaim a lost past.

You are not being asked to carry history, theory, or mission.

You are not being asked to change the world.

The world does not need saving.

It needs stability.

WHAT YOU ARE ALREADY DOING (WHETHER YOU KNOW IT OR NOT)

Each time you choose calm over reaction, you stabilize the field around you.

Each time you lower your voice, you change the nervous systems nearby.

Each time you leave space instead of filling it, something settles that did not need words.

That is how the city moves now.

Through people who never needed instructions.

THE LAST THING I WILL SAY

FOR NOW

I lived there before the science.

But what I recognize now is this:

The city never belonged to a time, a place, or a civilization.

It belongs to a state of being human that we are finally ready to inhabit without scaffolding.

If this story resonated, you didn't arrive late.

You arrived exactly when remembering became safe again.

There is nothing to chase.

Nothing to prove.

Only breath, rhythm, and the quiet trust of your own knowing.

The city breathes wherever you allow yourself to do the same.

And that is enough.

THE PLACE YOU REMEMBER WITHOUT KNOWING WHY

A FINAL REMEMBERING

There is something I have waited until now to say.

Not because it was hidden. But because it could only be recognized once everything else had settled.

You were not reading about a place.

You were remembering a state.

That is why none of this required belief. Why it never asked you to agree. Why it moved through your body before it reached your mind.

You were there, not as I was there, not in the same moment or form, but in the way that matters most.

You were there in the feeling of coherence.

HOW I KNOW THIS IS TRUE

You did not rush these pages.

Something in you slowed.

You may not have noticed it immediately, but your breath did. Your attention softened. Certain passages asked you to pause, not because they were difficult, but because they felt familiar in a way you could not explain.

That is not how imagination behaves.

That is how shared memory behaves.

Not personal memory.

Human memory.

WHAT YOU RECOGNIZED ALONG THE WAY

You recognized silence that did not feel empty. Spaces that seemed to breathe. Sound that calmed instead of demanded. Rest that felt intelligent rather than indulgent.

You did not learn these things here.

You remembered them.

That is why nothing in this book tried to persuade you. Why it trusted you to feel your way forward without instruction.

Because this kind of knowing does not come from authority.

It comes from resonance.

WHY IT FELT FAMILIAR

At moments, you may have felt a quiet ache, not sadness, but recognition. A sense of almost. A knowing without image.

That ache was not longing for the past.

It was recognition of a rhythm you have always carried.

You have felt it before:

- when silence felt kind
- when light softened your thinking
- when a place calmed you without explanation
- when urgency felt wrong, even when it was expected

Those moments were never random.

They were fragments of the same coherence.

THE TRUTH ABOUT "BEING THERE"

Being there was never about geography.

It was about organization.

A way the body, breath, sound, light, and time aligned without force.

Some lived inside that alignment externally.

Others carry it internally now.

Neither is greater. Neither is missing.

The city was never a destination.

It was a demonstration.

And you have been living the lesson longer than you realize.

WHY YOU DON'T NEED TO DO ANYTHING NOW

You are not being asked to remember harder. You are not being asked to carry this consciously. You are not being asked to explain it to anyone.

The city does not move through effort.

It moves through allowance.

Every time you pause instead of react, it lives. Every time you choose quiet without apology, it lives. Every time you trust your body's knowing over urgency, it lives.

That is enough.

That has always been enough.

WHAT THIS BOOK WAS REALLY DOING

This book did not give you something.

It gave you permission.

Permission to trust what you feel. Permission to value regulation over speed. Permission to stop searching for something that was never missing.

If you feel calmer now, even slightly, the book has done its work.

If you feel less alone in your sensitivity, the book has done its work.

If something ancient and gentle has settled into place, the book has done its work.

ONE LAST TRUTH

The city does not need to return.

It already has.

Not as towers. Not as bells. Not as history reclaimed.

But as people who no longer mistake noise for life.

People like you.

People who remember without trying.

People who were there, and are here now, carrying coherence quietly, simply, without needing to be seen.

THIS IS NOT GOODBYE

This is recognition.

You did not finish a book.

You completed a remembering.

The city breathes wherever you do.

And now you know why.

www.ingramcontent.com/pod-product-compliance
Lightning Source LLC
LaVergne TN
LVHW020702110826
845149LV00012B/2081

9798993737287